T0171684

The Life of
MAXINE HOLSINGER

MAXINE HOLSINGER

Order this book online at www.trafford.com
or email orders@trafford.com

Most Trafford titles are also available at major online book retailers.

Printed in the United States of America.

ISBN: 978-1-4907-1060-0 (sc)
ISBN: 978-1-4907-1059-4 (e)

Trafford rev. 11/09/2013

 www.trafford.com

North America & international
toll-free: 1 888 232 4444 (USA & Canada)
fax: 812 355 4082

PREFACE

I'm writing this book at the ripe old age of seventy-five. I will try to put in all relatives and friends as far as I can remember. I have been diagnosed with cancer (multiple myeloma), which is incurable at this time but can be treated. This book has been inspired by God, and since I am trying to be obedient, who knows what will happen. With him, all things are possible. I'm sure he will allow me to finish this book, but if not, God's will be done. I hope you will enjoy reading this book.

CHAPTER ONE

$\mathcal{I}$ was born in a small town in Rockingham County in the state of Virginia. My early life began in this area. I am the daughter of Earman and Madeline Roadcap. Madeline had a son by her first husband. This union was doomed from the beginning. David was a cruel man and very jealous of Mom. When he had to go away, he would lock her in the house until he returned. I never found out how she got away from him, but somehow, she managed to get away and divorce him. Years later, she married my dad. Daddy never accepted Maynard (my half brother) as his stepson, so he went off to live with my grandma, Mary Pittington (Mom's mother), until he joined the navy. Ten years later, Mom and Dad were blessed with a baby boy, Donald Roadcap (my full brother). We called him Donnie. He was the apple of Daddy's eye. Twenty-two months later, I was born. My younger sister hadn't been born yet. She is almost six years younger than me. They named her Emma. They knew she would be their last child since she was a change-of-life baby. Mom was about forty when Emma was born. Somehow, over the years, Emma began to develop a mental problem that was so mild, nobody seemed to notice, not even Mom and Dad, but I noticed.

CHAPTER TWO

When I was two and Donnie was four, they moved the family to Baltimore, Maryland. There was Daddy, Mama, Donnie, and me. We spent a short time in Maryland. During that time, I was a very headstrong child and thought I was bigger and older than I was. One day, Mom and Dad were taking us for a walk in the city. Baltimore was a busy city, with lots of traffic. I broke free from Mama's hand and ran as fast as I could run. Mom couldn't catch me as I started to dart out in the traffic. Fortunately, a man on the corner caught me and saved me from being hit by a car. They had to do something to control their headstrong little daughter, so they put a harness with a leash on me and led me around like a puppy. I really didn't mind. Anytime anybody wanted to take me anywhere, Mom always made sure I was in my harness. There was a teenage boy and a girl who lived nearby. They frequently came to pick me up and take me for snow cones. I looked forward to seeing them because I knew they would get me a snow cone. I got different flavors, but my favorite was cherry.

I continued to be a difficult child. I wanted to go with Daddy to take the car to the garage. Mom dressed me in my little blue silk dress. She always wanted me to look nice. She warned me before we left not to get dirty. I assured her she had nothing to worry about. Needless to say, I got black grease all over my pretty blue dress. I never could explain how that could have possibly happened.

When I was three and Donnie was five, Daddy was diagnosed with tuberculosis, which, in those days, was a life-threatening disease. Daddy was sent to Blue Ridge Sanatorium in Charlottesville, where he would be cared for. Mom got a sewing job at a factory in Charlottesville and got a very small apartment in a home with another family. She couldn't afford a babysitter on her meager salary, so the people in the house were kind enough to keep an eye on us. They had three boys, which gave Donnie playmates. I had nobody but Donnie and the boys. Donnie and the boys went off to play, and I was left alone in the apartment. Mom had a small white enamel table with four chairs and a two-burner stove in the kitchen, where she prepared decent meals for the three of us. While Donnie and the boys were out playing, I made sugar-bread sandwiches for Donnie's lunch. I climbed up on one of the chairs so I could reach the sugar bowl, which was in the middle of the table. I made a mean sugar-bread sandwich! The boys went home for their lunch while Donnie had sugar-bread sandwiches with me. Donnie and the boys went back out to play, and again, I was left alone. When Donnie and the boys came back, the boys brought me some pretty bottles and told me they were diamonds, each one of them trying to outdo the others. I took the bottles and treasured them as though they were real diamonds. Donnie told me he had crucified a worm and wanted me to go outside to see what he had done. I found a fishing worm nailed to a board. No big thing as far as I was concerned. After Donnie and the boys left, I was looking for something to get into. It didn't take long until I spotted Donnie's toy horn. I thought there has to be more you can do with a toy horn besides just blowing into it. I had already done that. I stuck my finger in the mouthpiece of the horn and got it stuck on my finger. Donnie came in and said, "Sissy, what have you done now?" He called me Sissy. He tried to pull the horn off my finger, but it wouldn't budge. There was nothing to do but wait until Mama got home. She could fix everything. She always did. She was a very strong woman. Mama came home, but by that time, my finger had swollen inside the horn. She tried to get it off, but it still wouldn't budge, so off to the hospital we went. They had to put me to sleep to cut the horn off. They got me all stitched up and sent me home with Mama and Donnie. Everything was fine except for my sore finger.

CHAPTER THREE

$\mathcal{M}$om was taking us to see Daddy. We couldn't go in because we were too young. We lay on the bank under Daddy's window. We would look up at the moon and stars, and Donnie would say, "I see the moon, and the moon sees me. God bless that there moon and God bless me." Daddy came to the window, looking out at us. He brought each one of us a little gift and lowered our gift on a string. We both got new pocket watches. We thought it was the best gift ever. The older boys at our apartment house taught us to tell time. We felt we had accomplished a lot from Daddy's gift. He thought so too since I was only three and Donnie was five.

CHAPTER FOUR

At another time when I was outside, playing by myself, I decided I was going to climb to the very top of the woodpile behind the house. It was a gorgeous day, and it seemed like it would be an interesting thing to do to climb to the very top. I didn't make it. I fell and hurt myself in my private area. I was hurting real bad. I didn't want Donnie to know about it, so I went in on the bed to try to stop hurting and pretended to be asleep. I thought, *I'll just stay here until Mama comes home. She'll fix it. Mom could fix anything.* When Mama came home, she asked Donnie where I was. Donnie told her I was sleeping. Mama came to check on me, and I told her what happened. She took one look at me, and off to the hospital we went again. They were trying to get me to pee. They held me over running water, hoping that would work. Nothing they tried seemed to work. They told Mom she could take me home, but if I hadn't gone until morning, she would have to bring me back. When morning came, she put me on my little pot and made me pee if I could or not. She told me to try real hard because she had to go to work. I strained and strained, and finally, I was able to go. It burned like crazy, but at least, Mama could go to work. I was feeling better later that day. Mama was happy, and so was I.

CHAPTER FIVE

*D*addy wasn't getting any better. The hospital had done all they could do for him, so they sent him home to die. Mom moved us back home to Daddy's mother and father's house in Singers Glen. Mom said. I went out in the field behind the house, picking daisies and singing, "I hope my daddy don't go dead. I hope my daddy don't die." I took the little bouquet to Daddy, who was sitting on an old car seat with a pencil and paper in his hand. Daddy prayed to the Lord to spare his life so he could watch his children grow up. He turned his life over to God and repented of his sins. While he was sitting on the car seat, he wrote a poem, which would later become a song. He wrote:

> One evening on my father's porch, I never will forget.
> All wracked with pain, my heart with fear that I began to fret.
> I cried, "Oh Lord, what can I do? I feel so bad, you see."

> I heard a voice say sweet and low, "Just have more
>   faith in me."
> I did that moment pray aloud, and Jesus heard my
>   prayer.
> He said that he would take my case, if I his love
>   would share.
> Today, as I go marching on, I know I have that
>   friend,
> Who will lead me to eternal life, where joy will
>   never end.

Daddy's health started to improve, and everybody knew that only God could do it. We were moving out of Grandma and Grandpap's house just up the road to a little house we rented from Earl Funk. Daddy got to know a preacher, Paul Frye, who began to come to our house to hold prayer meetings. Paul and his wife, Sadie, had a daughter they called Paula. We soon became best friends although she was four years older than me. Daddy finally got strong enough to attend Paul Frye's church in Harrisonburg. He took us to church and also had prayer meetings in our home. I learned to sing harmony with Daddy at the age of four. We sang the song Daddy had written. I also sang harmony with Paula. There was a taxi company at the back of the church called Powell's Taxi. There was a small door between Powell's Taxi and the church. Mr. Powell would open that door so he could hear those Holy Rollers sing. We were making a joyful noise unto the Lord. Mr. Powell sometimes opened the door wide so he could not only hear but also see what we were doing. We attended church three times during the week and also had prayer meetings in our home.

CHAPTER SIX

At this time, I was four and Donnie was six. Donnie had just started school with our cousins. They lived up the hill on the right side of our little house. They were the children of Uncle John and Aunt Daisy. We always played with Uncle John's children. Jean was older than me, but Bobby was about Donnie's age. They were having a Christmas program at school, and Santa was going to be there. Jean asked Mom and Dad if she could take me to school that day. They said I could go. I was so excited I could hardly wait. That made me feel like a big girl now. I was going to school with my cousin Jean and also my big brother, Donnie. I was only four years old, but in my mind, I was as old as Jean and Donnie were. I had a wonderful time at school. Santa had given me candy and an orange. We got on the bus and were on our way home when I dropped my orange. It had been too calm during the day, so I needed to create a little drama—not much, just a little bit. The orange rolled to the back of the bus and out a hole at the wheel of the bus. Jean asked the bus driver to stop so she could retrieve my orange. Jean got my orange and got back on the bus, and we were on our way home again. I thanked Jean for taking me and getting my orange back. I told her how much I enjoyed school.

CHAPTER SEVEN

We continued to live in the little house when Emma was born. Paul Frye, our pastor, brought Mama home with Baby Emma. Donnie and I were thrilled to have a baby sister. She was as cute as a button, and I loved her from the get-go. It was quite a struggle for Mom since she had to take a leave from work to have the baby. Friends from church brought us groceries; and Ruth, Uncle John's daughter, offered to adopt me. She was grown and married to her first husband, and they had no children. Mama told her she appreciated the offer, but she just couldn't let me go regardless of the problems I caused her at times. Daddy was doing much better, but he still had to go to the doctor to have fluid drawn off his lungs. They put a long needle in his side to draw out the fluid. It was very painful. They didn't have the kind of painkillers that we have now. When he came home from seeing the doctor, I would rub him down with alcohol and put powder on him. Mama went back to work to support the family. We continued to have prayer meetings in our home and go to the same church. Mamie Ray lived up the road from my grandparents, and she would come every now and then to play with me. We were the same age. We would go up in the woods and play house. The pretty green moss was our carpet, and we used acorns for our cups and saucers. We also made mud pies. I tried to get Mamie to eat my mud pies, but she wouldn't do it. I still liked her even if she wouldn't eat my mud pies. We went up to Uncle John's a lot. Hessie, Uncle John's oldest daughter, gave me a little china doll about an inch or more tall. I still have that little doll to this day. Uncle John's girls had a lot of interesting things. They had some wooden Dutch shoes that I thought were neat. They let me clomp around in them.

CHAPTER EIGHT

$\mathcal{D}$addy said we were going to move from our little house next to Uncle John's. I was very unhappy because I didn't want to leave my cousins. We were moving to a house near Mount Clinton. We rented a house from John Myers. We lived close to an old feed mill called Stultz's Mill. Donnie and I would go down to the mill and drink cider right out of the hose. We had a billy goat we called Billy. Donnie made a little cart to pull behind the goat. I wanted to try the cart out, so Donnie hitched Billy to the cart, and off we went. We didn't get very far before Billy dumped me in a sinkhole. The bottom of the sinkhole was full of rocks. I walked away with just a few scratches and a bruise or two. I was pretty tough. Donnie was eight, and I was six. Emma was still a small baby. My first grade started at Mount Clinton. I cried the first day because I missed Mama and Daddy. The teachers got together and brought Donnie down to stay with me the first day. Donnie was used to going to school, but this was something new for me. The second day of school, I was still wearing white baby shoes that Mama had gotten from welfare. They didn't give out much in those days, and the shoes fit me, so that's what I had to wear. Of course, I didn't want to look like a baby. After all, I thought I was really a big girl now, going to school with my big brother. I was really upset about those shoes, so Daddy told me he would dye them black. I thought that was a very good idea, and I was very happy about having black shoes. While Daddy was polishing the shoes, he spilled the polish. I thought, *Oh no! Now I would have to wear one black shoe and one white shoe to school.* Daddy managed to save the day and was able to scrape up enough polish to polish the other shoe, so I was happy again. Every day, when I came home from school, I would train Billy. I was very determined I was going to make that goat listen to me. Finally, I got him trained, and I would hitch him up to the little cart and drive him across the road to the Showalters' house. Mom bought milk from them, and Billy and I would go pick it up. Now I was driving. I may have been driving a goat instead of a car, but I was driving.

The Showalter woman came to our house to seed cherries. I was helping them when all of a sudden everything started getting black in front of my eyes. Mama told me I said Mama I and passed out. I was going to say "Mama I'm sick", but before I could get the words out of my mouth, I was out. We never found out what caused me to pass out. The only thing I knew was when I woke up, they were washing my face with a wash cloth. They didn't take you to the doctor for every little thing in those days because they always thought God would take care of it and He did, because I'm still here trying to write this book.

CHAPTER NINE

$\mathcal{B}$efore Donnie and I started school again, we moved just outside the city of Harrisonburg called the Gains Place. We were having supper and had a watermelon that evening. Emma had hollowed out the center, which was the best part. She was such a little pig. Whenever we had anything good to eat, she would scarf up most of it before Donnie and I got any. I thought I needed to teach that little twerp a lesson, so I took her out to the smokehouse, where they kept a big container of lard. I told her the lard was ice cream and gave her a big spoonful of it. She gulped it down in no time flat, but then she started gagging and carrying on. She won't use lard for anything to this day. We attended Pleasant Hill School. Then the landlord sold the house, but he had a tenant house behind the big house, so we moved in to that. I thought that was very good because we wouldn't have to change schools, especially this soon. I was in third grade now, and Donnie was in fifth. This was where Daddy started drinking wine. Mama grabbed his wine bottle, and they went round and round, struggling over that wine bottle. He said it was just a little wine. The Bible even said to drink it for your stomach's sake. I remember, while they were struggling over the wine, they shot that red wine all over the walls, floors, and everything. The house was a mess. Not to worry, we were moving again. This time, we still wouldn't change schools because we were just moving down on Route 11 where Mom and Dad were going to operate a little business for Mr. Liskey. They would also be renting cabins for overnight guests. Mom sold groceries, candies, and drinks in the store; and Daddy pumped gas. Mama always kept records of everything. This store was later known as Hillcrest. Donnie and I used to walk to Harrisonburg, picking up pop bottles along the way and selling them at Spitzer's store. If we had enough money, we went to the movies. We got two cents for each bottle. We had to pick up a lot of bottles to pay for both of us to go to the movies. The movies cost twenty-two cents each, so we had to have forty-four cents. We did real well most of the time, but when we didn't have enough to go to the movies, we just bought candy and went back home. We went to the movies almost every Saturday. We usually watched Westerns with Roy Rogers and Dale Evans, Red Ryder and Little Beaver, Tex Ritter, and Gene Autry (the singing cowboy). We also watched cartoons and news flicks. If we had a really good day selling our bottles, we could even get popcorn to share. We still attended church on Wednesday, Saturday, and Sunday nights. It was a Pentecostal church. People called us Holy Rollers. It was very strict, and we had to abide by the rules. At that time, the Greyhound bus station was just up from the church. The front of the bus station faced Main Street. The back was up from the church. Donnie and I were allowed to go up to the bus station when we got restless in church because the services went on and on and on. We were each given a nickel to spend. We always bought cherry smashes. Then we would go back to the church and wait for Mama, Daddy, and Emma.

CHAPTER TEN

$\mathcal{T}$here was a lady who lived down the street from our store. Her name was Mrs. Harpine. She had heart problems, and she needed somebody to help her with the housework and laundry. She couldn't afford to pay a regular cleaning lady, so she thought of me. She had heard I was a good worker and helped Mom all the time, so she hired me. At that time, I had a little scooter I bought for myself, making a little money here and there and saving all I could. I had my eye on that little scooter. It was between a red and an orange in color and had a seat and a brake on it. I saved a very long time to buy it, but I was determined I was going to get that scooter. I finally had enough money to buy it. Since Harrisonburg wasn't that far away from our store, I walked to pick up my scooter. I rode my scooter back home. I also rode my scooter to work for Mrs. Harpine. I could coast down the hill to her house and sit on my little seat, and if I started to go too fast, I would put on my brake. I would park my scooter beside her house, just like a car. I was driving again. This time, I was driving a scooter instead of a goat. Mrs. Harpine was pleased with my work. I didn't get to finish third grade before we were moving again. *Oh no! Not again.* Daddy told me he would still bring me in to work for Mrs. Harpine, so I felt much better because I didn't want to let her down. We had gotten very close while I worked for her. She really appreciated having me there.

CHAPTER ELEVEN

This time, we moved to Keezletown. We lived in a house they called the Billy House. I finished my third grade at Keezletown. Then we had summer break. Daddy had started drinking and smoking now. We were still going to the same church, and Daddy was a saint in church, but when we were home, he turned into a real devil. I looked more like my half brother, Maynard, than I did my real siblings. I think Daddy resented me because I looked like Maynard, and he knew Maynard didn't belong to him. He accused Mama right in front of me that I wasn't his daughter. I knew better than that. I knew Mama was a saint, and she had nothing to hide. She was always the same sweet and kind person in church or out of church. Unlike him, she was a real Christian. Now with his warped mind, it was hard to know what he was thinking. I had been reading the passage in the Bible where it said, "Ye must be hot or cold or I'll spew you out of my mouth." Daddy was headed down this path. One evening, when Mom and I were washing dishes, Daddy came in drunk and picked up our dishpan full of dishes and threw them out in the yard. He broke a lot of Mom's good dishes. This was the last straw for Mom. She had been putting up with his bad behavior for a long time. She grabbed me by the hand and started walking. I asked her where we were going, and she said, "Harrisonburg." I asked why she didn't bring Donnie and Emma. She said because she knew Daddy would be good to them. She knew he would be mean to me because in his mind, I didn't belong to him any more than Maynard did. I knew Mama was a good woman and would never ever cheat on Daddy. She was an angel to me. We didn't get very far before Daddy caught us and forced us to get in the car. Then he took off like a possessed man, which I knew he was. He was possessed by the devil. I was really scared, and so was Mama. I prayed that the Lord would protect us, and he answered my prayer. Mama said, "Are you trying to kill us? Do you hate us that much?" He finally slowed down, and we made it back home safely. After Daddy sobered up, we went back to church. Nobody knew what was going on at home. I knew Daddy was living a lie, and I never trusted him after that, but I still loved him and continued to pray for him. I never told anybody what Daddy had done. Not even my best friend, Paula. I was so ashamed of the way he was acting. He only acted that way when he was drunk, but he was getting drunk more often. He seemed to forget what God had done for him.

CHAPTER TWELVE

$\mathcal{I}$ was nine years old when I accepted Jesus as my Savior. I was baptized in the river, and when I came up, I felt totally renewed. We kept going to church, and I kept singing with Daddy and Paula. I refused to sing with Daddy once, and I paid for it. I didn't want to sing with him because I knew it wasn't real. Things had changed so much, and Daddy was living a double life. I felt sad but still rejoiced in the Lord. He would always take care of me. I had a heavenly Father who loved me even if my earthly father didn't. I prayed for Mama because I knew she was hurting too. The Lord was merciful to Daddy and forgave him time after time. I loved the Lord so much, and I knew he loved me more. Daddy moved us again but to a better house in Keezletown. We rented from Charlie Raines and his wife. They had children, both boys and girls, but Ellen was my favorite playmate. I would go over to Ellen's, and we would play basketball. We usually played follow the leader, and we had to hit every basket the leader did. I had lost to Ellen the last time we played, so now she was the leader. If we missed a basket, we were a rotten egg, and the other person would become the leader. Ellen missed her basket, and I got all excited and yelled, "You is him! You is him!" meaning she was the rotten egg. She teased me about that for weeks. After Ellen and I finished playing, her dad, Charlie, would always take me home, with me riding behind him on their old mule. We lived just over the hill from them. I always looked forward to my ride on the mule. I almost liked my ride on the mule as much as I liked playing basketball with Ellen.

CHAPTER THIRTEEN

$\mathcal{M}$om and Dad received a telegram from my half brother, Maynard. It said, "Arriving home with bride, arrival time unknown." When Maynard came home with his bride, I realized she was pregnant. I later learned that the baby didn't belong to Maynard. I knew Maynard either was drunk or felt sorry for the woman. I didn't know which. Her maiden name was Jean Hill, and she was from Knoxville, Tennessee. Of course, she was now Jean Hasler.

Maynard had to get back to the ship, and Jean was staying with us. Maynard paid Daddy, and they worked it all out. The baby was born, and she named him Maynard Hasler Jr. He was so cute. I loved him right away. Daddy even loved baby Woodie, as we called him later on because he had red hair and reminded you of a little woodpecker. Daddy loved Woodie so much you would have thought he was his father. I was glad. I thought this would help Daddy stop drinking. Not so. He continued to drink. One day, Donnie was pestering Woodie, and Jean got real mad. She didn't like Donnie anyhow. She walked over to the table, picked up an ashtray, emptied the ashes in the stove, and proceeded to hit Donnie over the head with the ashtray. He was bleeding real bad. I quickly got a towel and wet it with cold water and put it around Donnie's head to try to stop the bleeding. Then Mom and Dad came home from work. Dad rushed Donnie to the hospital to find she had cracked his skull. Dad had Jean arrested. She had to take Woodie with her because she was nursing at that time. Jean and Woodie spent the night in jail. Little Woodie was totally innocent, yet he had become a jailbird. The next day, Daddy bailed her out, I think mostly because he wanted to get Woodie out. Otherwise, she would have stayed in there a very long time. After a while, Jean started getting restless. After the thing with Donnie, I'm sure she felt rejected by the family. She said she was going back to her hometown in Knoxville, Tennessee. I don't remember how long she was gone, but she was gone for quite some time. When she called and asked if she could come back, we were all overjoyed. We all missed little Woodie so much. Daddy was really glad to have Woodie back. He loved him like he loved a son and was very proud of him. Even Donnie and Emma loved Woodie. When they came back, Woodie was on a bottle now and would hold it with his hands and feet like a little monkey would. He also had the rickets. I didn't even know what rickets were. Mom slowly got him back to health with the help of God and the doctors.

CHAPTER FOURTEEN

We visited Uncle John and Aunt Daisy frequently. The two families stayed very close. I was so happy when we went back to Uncle John's. I missed them so much. Although we visited very often, it just wasn't the same as having them next door. My sister was always showing off at Uncle John's, trying to get everybody's attention, so I decided to write a little poem about her. I wrote:

> I have a little sister who likes to attract attention,
> But some of the things she does, I wouldn't dare to
>   mention.
> She usually sings or dances; she knows she's good
>   at it,
> But whenever she gets started, she doesn't know
>   when to quit.
> People like to hear her songs when she only sings
>   a few,
> But they are good and tired of it by the time that
>   she gets through.

She can dance to a waltz; she can also dance the
    polka,
And I hear a lot of people say she looks like
    Imogene Coca.

CHAPTER FIFTEEN

*J*ean was getting restless again and wanted to go back to Tennessee. Woodie was just getting better, and things were looking up. Now Jean is going to take Woodie again. I know Mom and I prayed for Woodie, not only for his health, but also because we didn't want Jean to take him again. Jean said she wouldn't be taking Woodie this time. I knew for certain that God had answered our prayers. I was nine and Donnie was eleven and Emma was three. Daddy said he thought I was old enough to take care of baby Woodie and Emma. He said Donnie was old enough to fend for himself. Daddy said he would give me a small allowance for doing this. I think it was $5 each week. I agreed to that, so I became babysitter and housekeeper. I was still working for Mrs. Harpine. Daddy said he would keep driving me in on Saturdays to help her, and since Mama would be home with the kids, it would work out fine. This sounded like a good plan to me.

CHAPTER SIXTEEN

$\mathcal{M}$y grandmother Mary snow lived just up the road from us, and we visited her from time to time. This time, I got to visit with my first cousin Betty Jean. Aunt Lizzy, as I called her, was Mom's sister and Betty Jean's mother. I didn't know why Grandma was taking care of Betty Jean. I only knew she was there and I would have somebody to play with. Betty Jean had a whole lot of dolls, and she let me play with all of them. I thought I was in heaven because I only had one doll. After we visited Grandma for a while, we went on up the road where Marion and Becky lived. I can remember Becky because she would grab me and give me a great, big hug and pinch my cheeks until they hurt, but she didn't mean to hurt me. She would say, "You are the cutest little thing." I didn't think I was cute, but I thanked Becky for the compliment anyhow. We used to just go visit people. I don't know why we don't still visit. Everybody is just too busy.

CHAPTER SEVENTEEN

We were all getting older. Donnie was turning twelve, I was ten, and Emma was four. Daddy had a secondhand shop in Harrisonburg, and he would take each one of us with him now and then. Today happened to be my day to go. I was with Daddy the day Pauline's beauty shop exploded. We could see it all from the secondhand store. I remember there was a blacksmith shop across the street. The man who owned the blacksmith shop went running out to see what was going on. It so happened that one of our neighbor's daughters was going to cosmetology school there. She was killed in the explosion. Her name was Bonnie Sites. She was a beautiful girl. I remember going to see her in her casket. She looked like an angel. She was dressed in a pale blue dress. I thought she was too young to die. She had her whole life ahead of her, so I thought. That is the reason it's so important to stay close to God, because we don't have to be old to die.

CHAPTER EIGHTEEN

$\mathcal{I}$ continued to take care of things at home, which now included washing, ironing, and cooking. After all, I was ten now, and I could handle the extra work. Mama appreciated it. She didn't ask me to do it. I liked helping Mom. She was tired in the evening and really needed a helping hand. I also thought about what she went through for me when I was growing up. I dearly loved Mama, but I was still afraid of Daddy, especially when he was drunk. I would just try to stay out of his way. Daddy was doing a little better lately but was still living his lie in church. One day, when I was home with the kids, we were getting a real bad thunderstorm. We were all afraid, including Donnie. I called Daddy on the phone, and he closed the shop and came home. The storm subsided, and Daddy went back to work. He also had to pick up Mama. The summer was over, and we had to start back to school. Mom and Dad had to make other arrangements about a babysitter and cleaning lady for Emma and Woodie. Now I would be back in school. I would be starting fourth grade this year. My teacher was Mrs. Burtner. I didn't like her a little bit.

She had taught my daddy, and she was getting old and cranky. I was glad to get out of her class. My fifth-grade teacher was Mrs. Koontz, and I really liked her. She gave us an assignment to write a poem about the first day of spring I had no problem with making things rhyme. I wrote...

The First Day Of Spring

This is the first day of spring when the robins begin
 to sing,
And the trees are getting green, This would please a
 Queen.
The little flowers are so gay dancing about all the day,
I will ask it if I may, Why can't spring always stay?
I certainly would like to know why can't warm
 winds always blow?
It hasn't been so long ago since the ground was
 covered with snow,
Now the grass is beginning to grow and the warm
 waters beginning to flow,
The birds are singing so sweet and low, I just wish it
 would never snow.

I got an A for my poem. Believe it or not, we were still living in the same house, and I was going to the same school. That was where I met Jerry Shull. As I recall, he was a very nice boy with wavy blond hair. I now go to church with him and his wife, Louetta. There was another boy in my class who wasn't so nice. His name was Billy Viger. He picked on me constantly. I had enough of this Viger kid, so I dared him out on the playground at recess. When recess came, Billy was there, but there was also one of my friends, Jiggs Dorman, and he was carrying a big stick in case I needed any help. I didn't think I would need him because I was pretty tough from fighting with my brother, Donnie. I stepped closer to him and told him to give me his best shot. He hit me in the face, but that didn't faze me. Now it was my turn. I lit into him and whipped him good. Needless to say, he stopped picking on me and kept his distance from me. While I was still in fifth grade, there were going to be some people going to our school to make a movie of the school. At least we were going to be a part of it. Mrs. Koontz picked me to point out things on the globe with a pointer she had given me. I think she picked me because I was the smallest kid in the class, and she wanted them to think I was smart. She sure fooled them. I did my little thing there with the pointer, and we all went out to play. It was recess. Later on, they were going to show a preview of the movie at school. Charles Raines asked me if I would like to go with him and his girlfriend. I said, "Sure." We were seated in the auditorium to watch the movie. I was never so shocked in all my life when I saw myself not only at the globe with my pointer but also on the playground—on the monkey bars, the swings, and the seesaws—I was all over the place. I didn't know this before I saw the movie. I didn't see anybody when I was on the playground. I thought, *Those sneaky people. Why didn't I see them anywhere?* We were headed home, and Charles was teasing me about being the star of the show. It started snowing, and that got his mind on something besides the movie. I got excited about the snow. The flakes were getting bigger and bigger. I just kept looking at them coming down until it made me dizzy. When we got home, I thanked Charles for taking me and told him I enjoyed it. Maybe not so much after I found out I was in it as much as I was. After my fifth grade of school, Daddy informed us that we were moving again. We were going back to Singers Glen. It wasn't very close to my cousins, but at least, we were back in the area.

CHAPTER NINETEEN

We moved to a house across from the cemetery where Daddy is now buried. I think the house is now an electronic shop. Dad bought this house. We were no longer renting. There was still a family living there, but Dad worked out an arrangement with them so we could go ahead and move. They were in the process of moving out, and we were in the process of moving in. They had a girl about my age of twelve. Donnie was fourteen, and Emma was six. She would be starting first grade in the fall. Dad wanted to get us all settled before school started again. The bus would be picking us up right in front of the house. We wouldn't have to walk a mile like Donnie and I had to do when we lived at the Billy House in Keezletown. Donnie put water on his hair, and by the time we got to the bus stop, it was frozen stiff. Now we could stay in the house and see when the bus stopped up the road to pick up the Stroop kids. By the time they loaded the Stroop kids, it was time for us to walk out our front door. This was much better than before when Donnie had a habit of licking his tongue around his mouth. He always had a ring where it had chapped most of the winter. Now we could stay in where it was nice and warm until the bus came. Here at Singers Glen, we could walk to school when it was nice outside. When I walked, I would ask Betty Euing to walk with me. She lived just up the road from the Stroops. She usually walked with me. Our plan was that we would stop by Emmer Lee's store and buy candy on our way home. Emmer Lee's also served as a post office. I was in sixth grade now, Donnie was in seventh, and Emma was in first grade. There were two classes in the same room, which put me and Donnie together for the first time. Mrs. Tucker was our teacher. She was also the principal, art teacher, and music teacher. She turned out to be my favorite teacher. I admired her for all her talents, and I learned to love her very much, but she was a challenge to me. I wanted to be just like Mrs. Tucker, which I achieved in most areas except art. I couldn't draw a lick. Later on you will see I finally achieved that too. In sixth grade, I had to sit in the same desk with Shelby Funk. We became friends right away. Shelby and I used to sing for devotions. She sang soprano, and of course, I sang alto. I sometimes sang with another girl, named Frankie Knight. I was really enjoying school at Singers Glen. No boys to fight with or anything, with the exception of my brother, Donnie. He pushed my buttons. Then Donnie started bringing different boys home to spend the night. They really liked me, and I think that's the reason they came home with Donnie. I didn't like any of them. I liked them but not the way they wanted me to, so I just stayed out of their way.

CHAPTER TWENTY

$\mathcal{N}$ext, I will tell you about my first puppy love. There was a preacher coming to Harrisonburg with a big tent, which held more people than I had seen in my life. We were able to attend the meetings every night. This helped Daddy because he wasn't drinking. He was still smoking. I thought he would do a turnaround and be the kind of dad I knew who loved me. I hadn't had that for a very long time. The first night, Daddy and I were scheduled to sing. I was real nervous because this was my first time to sing in front of so many people. We were singing with microphones for the first time. I had no idea how to turn them on. Daddy didn't know anything about them either, so Brother McKay had to turn them on for us. Brother McKay had a wife named Edith. She had come from a town in Canada called Eekin Seekin Bridge, Halifax, Nova Scotia, Canada. They had two nephews with them. They were Tommy and Walter McNeely. Tommy was close to Donnie's age, and Walter was closer to mine. They also had another couple with them who helped set up the tent and equipment. Of course, some of the people from our church helped too. Tommy played the sax, and Walter played a big bass horn. Daddy and I finally got through our song. We sang "Stepping in the Light." That was one of the favorites our congregation liked to hear us sing. Then Sister McKay gave a testimony, and Brother McKay brought the message. I enjoyed the service very much after Daddy and I finished our part. Then at the very end, Tommy and Walter played a horn duet. They were very good, and I enjoyed it very much. Maynard was home on leave, and he and his girlfriend, Mabel Stroop, who lived up the road from us, came in a separate car. They came because they knew that Daddy and I would be singing. Maynard was still drinking, but he was sober that night. Daddy had warmed up some to Maynard because Maynard paid Daddy to stay at the house while he was home on furlough. He also brought gifts for all of us and even bought his girlfriend a nice dress to wear to the church service. Maynard had such a good heart. His main drawback was his drinking.

CHAPTER TWENTY-ONE

$\mathcal{T}$he service was over, and we were starting to go home, when Tommy and Walter stopped me on the way out and told me they enjoyed our singing. I thanked them and told them I enjoyed their horn duet. Then I headed for the car. I greeted some of the church members on my way out, and I thought we were going home. When I got to the car, Daddy and Mama were seated up front and Emma was in the back-right corner. I slid in the back beside Emma, but Donnie was missing. Maynard and Mabel had already left. Donnie finally came out, and he had Walter with him. He asked Daddy if Walter could spend the night. Daddy said yes. He always welcomed our friends, but I was wondering why he brought Walter instead of Tommy because Tommy was more his age. Walter slid in next to me with that big bass horn on his lap. Donnie got in last. It didn't take me long to realize that Donnie was up to his old tricks. I had been through this so many times before; however, this time was different. Donnie did very well this time. I actually liked Walter in the way he wanted me to. Walter and I were in deep conversation, and Donnie sat quietly, listening to every word we said. Walter was a very good-looking boy. He had black hair and a gorgeous smile. He also dressed nicely. I'm sure you have guessed by now that Walter was about to become my first puppy love. The next day, Walter and I went for a walk up the hill and into the orchard. Curtis Ward was there too, but we didn't know he was there. Curtis liked me, but I didn't like him in the same way. This was where I got my first kiss on the lips. About that time, we spotted Curtis. He had been watching us the whole time. Walter said, "Did you see heaven?" Curtis was upset with me and Walter and stormed off. Walter and I went back to the house to join the rest of the family. Nobody knew what was going on between me and Walter. That night, we were off again to the tent meeting. Daddy and I were supposed to sing again. I wasn't as nervous this time. Sister McKay had brought Walter a fresh set of clothes, and he was changing in the back of the tent where they kept supplies and extra equipment. Daddy and I would be singing "Some Golden Daybreak." Walter came out from changing clothes, and Daddy and I were ready to sing. Then just like last night, Sister McKay gave her testimony. Tommy and Walter did their horn duet, and Brother McKay brought the message. He also had a healing service while we sang "Where the Healing Waters Flow." After the healing service, he gave the altar call, and many people came to the Lord. We were drawing bigger and bigger crowds every night. Walter stayed with us all week, and his aunt Edith would bring him a fresh change of clothes.

CHAPTER TWENTY-TWO

William and Edith McKay and the rest of the team were heading out for Baltimore, Maryland. Daddy told them we used to live there and would really like to go back. Those were the happy days before he got sick. Of course, the McKays wanted us to go. Before they left, Walter gave me a little Brownie camera. I was wondering how he managed to get that because he was at our house all week. I'm sure his aunt Edith got it for him to give to me. By now, everybody knew that Walter and I had something going. Daddy said that as much as he wanted to go, he just didn't have the money for the trip. Daddy was trying to think of something he could sell so we could go. He said he could sell our old cow, and that would give us enough money to make the trip. I prayed that daddy would sell that cow. Daddy sold the cow. We packed the car and took our little dog (Snookie) with us. The McKays and the boys had already been there two days. We were going to stay at the Biltmore Hotel, which was a very nice hotel, and dogs weren't allowed. Somehow, Daddy talked the manager into letting us keep Snookie in the hotel. When we first walked in the lobby, Walter was there, and when he saw us, his eyes got as big as saucers. He ran over and gave me a great, big hug. We had to check in, and we were given a room right off the lobby in case we needed help with Snookie. This room had five single beds in it—just perfect for us. We were ready to go to the service that night, but we didn't know what we were going to do with Snookie. The girls at the desk fell in love with little Snookie, so they offered to take care of her. Now we were ready to go. Of course, Brother McKay asked if we would sing that night. Daddy accepted. The service was a repeat of what we did in Harrisonburg, with an even bigger crowd. I wasn't nervous because I was getting used to doing this, and furthermore, I was in puppy love big-time. After church that night, Donnie, Walter, and I were allowed to ride the streetcars. Daddy, Mama, and Emma had gone back to the hotel and picked up Snookie. When we returned to the hotel, Walter went up to their room, and Donnie and I went to ours but not before we made plans for the next day. When Donnie and I got to the room, Mama was having an awful time with Daddy. He had gotten some of those little shot bottles of whiskey, and he was dead drunk. Mama said, "Deed-n-double, Earman, can't you stay sober while we're here?" *Deed-n-double* was Mama's byword. She used it all the time, especially when she was upset with Daddy. I was thanking God that Walter didn't come in with us. By the next day, Mama had gotten Daddy sobered up, and Donnie and I met Walter for breakfast. We spent that day together and had the same routine that night at church. The next morning, we all said our final good-byes. Walter hugged me and gave me a box of candy, which I shared with Donnie and Emma, but my and Walter's puppy love was far from over. We continued to write to each other, and Walter would send me little gifts in the mail.

CHAPTER TWENTY-THREE

While we were at Singers Glen, we had a spare room that Daddy said I could have to myself if I would paint that room and also paint their bedroom, which was across the hall from what was going to be my room. I gladly accepted this. I was getting tired of being cooped up with Emma, and it would also give her more space. Donnie already had a room of his own. It didn't need painting. The walls in his room were made of wood. I painted my room pink, and Dad and Mom's room blue. Emma's room was also made of wood, just like Donnie's. Emma's room used to be mine too.

CHAPTER TWENTY-FOUR

We went back home to Singers Glen, and all three of us had to go back to school. Woodie was the only one at home. Since Daddy and Mama were working and I was in school, they had to hire somebody to stay with Woodie. The woman I remember most was Hattie Bear. She had a small daughter, Catherine. She may have been a little older than Woodie. Hattie used to make the best vegetable soup I had ever tasted. She knew I loved her soup, so she made it often. I really liked Hattie, and she liked me and Woodie, but she didn't care for Donnie and Emma. Emma was starting first grade. They had two grades in the same room at Singers Glen School. Emma went to her first-grade class. Donnie and I went down the hall to our sixth—and seventh-grade class. This is the first time Donnie and I had ever been in the same room. Donnie and I kept getting into mischief at school. We went off the school property without permission and took a couple of friends along with us. We sat in somebody's yard next to the school. Mrs. Tucker, our teacher, caught us and made us write "I must obey the rules" five hundred times. Being the little mischievous brat that I was, I wrote mine with two pencils so I could finish in half the time. Every now and then, I would even throw in "I mustn't obey the rules." Mrs. Tucker either didn't catch it or let me get away with it. I don't know which. Then Donnie got the bright idea to build a fort on the clay bank behind the school, and we were going to play cowboys and Indians. Most of the school was participating. The school really didn't have that many students since there were two grades in the same room. Things were going real good, and most of us were out of the teachers' hair. We played in the fort for weeks until Donnie got another bright idea—he set the fort on fire. He almost got expelled from school for this little prank. Daddy went over and talked to Mrs. Tucker, who lived in the Glen. Mrs. Tucker played different roles in school. She was very talented and became my favorite teacher. She was the principal, art teacher, and music teacher. I admired her so very much. At this time, she was very angry with Donnie for what he had done. After Daddy talked to her, she calmed down. She was the principal, so she could have expelled Donnie. At least, Donnie wouldn't get expelled.

CHAPTER TWENTY-FIVE

$\mathcal{D}$addy was selling the house, and we were moving again. We were moving back to the same house we lived in when I was six. Back to Mr. Myers's, back to where I started first grade and had my goat, Billy. I never could understand why we were always moving. This time, Aunt Meg (Daddy's aunt) was moving with us. Aunt Meg was moving from Harrisonburg. We had visited her many times. She was a very vulgar old woman, and I didn't like being around her. By this time, Donnie had gotten his driver's license, and Daddy had bought him an old car. Since Donnie was driving, he could drive us all to school at Singers Glen, so we would be going to the same school. Actually, it wasn't that far from our house in Mount Clinton to Singers Glen School. Donnie and I sat in the front seat and Emma in the back. There were a lot of bumps in the road. Donnie liked to drive fast over those bumps, and that gave us all a thrill, especially Emma, who was in the backseat. One morning, Donnie was going extra fast over our favorite bump and bounced the car chains out of the trunk of the car. Emma got sick at school, and they put her in the music room, where they put the kids if they were sick. She probably got sick from going over those bumps and giggling herself silly. When I found out that she was in the music room all by herself, I knew I couldn't let that go on, so I pretended to be sick. Mrs. Tucker probably thought that I had come down with the same thing that Emma had. I opened the door to the music room, and when I walked in, Emma started grinning from ear to ear. It was really boring in that old music room, and I told her all the funny stories I could make up. I knew they kept costumes in the closet of the music room when we had plays at school. I put on one of the costumes and came back to entertain her. She liked that and seemed to be feeling much better. It was about time for the bell to ring for us to go home. I stashed the costumes back in the closet and jumped back in bed. Donnie had already gone to the car by the time we got out. We were on our way home over the bumps again, but Donnie wasn't driving as fast this time. It was still fast enough to give us a thrill.

CHAPTER TWENTY-SIX

$\mathcal{I}$ came up with something I thought I might try at school. We were doing writing tests. Every time we went to town, I bought ink in various colors. I thought this might add a little flare to the writing tests. They sold red, blue, and black ink in the store, so I bought one of each and started mixing them. I mixed red and black and got burgundy; blue and red made a nice shade of purple. I also had the basic colors of black, blue, and red. I was all set except for the mistakes I might make on my writing tests, so I had to come up with something to fix that problem. I knew Mom used Clorox to take stains out of clothes, so I thought that might work to take ink off the paper. I filled a Mercurochrome bottle with Clorox. With the little dabber that came with it, I could erase all my mistakes. I practiced at home to get it right. I had to be very careful and use very little Clorox so I wouldn't erase the lines off my paper. After I corrected the mistakes, I would go back after the Clorox was completely dry and do the part I had corrected, and you couldn't see that I had made any mistakes at all. I handed in perfect papers every time. Mrs. Tucker lined them up on the bulletin board in the different colors. I'm sure she knew what I was doing. She seemed to be impressed with this. After all, she was an art teacher and appreciated a little color. One day, the superintendent of schools visited our school, and she showed him all my papers. I couldn't hear what they were saying, but I knew she was proud of me because she was smiling that certain kind of smile when she was pleased. The superintendent was smiling too. After that, my classmates started noticing my writing papers with the colorful ink. I continued to buy more ink every time I went to town. I was beginning to run out of small bottles to put my mixed ink in. I was always in demand for small bottles. Mom was saving all she could for me, so for now, I had an adequate supply. Now I was trading bottles of ink for all kinds of neat stuff from my classmates. If they brought me small bottles, I would compensate them by giving them extra ink. My favorite thing I traded for was a big Bible storybook. I still have that book. It has aged a lot because it's been a long time since I got it.

We used to play truth or consequences in school, and the kids always wanted Mrs. Tucker to dance a jig as her consequence. She could cut a rug. She had such tiny legs, I had to wonder how they held her up. One day, some of my classmates and I were in the music room and I was showing off for them. I was dancing a jig like Mrs. Tucker's when she walked into the room. Mrs. Tucker said, "That's very good, Maxine."

CHAPTER TWENTY-SEVEN

$\mathcal{T}$he following school year, Donnie and I would be going to Linville Edom School, which was a high school. We met the Linville Edom bus at Singers Glen School. Donnie and I did fine because we would just be transferred to Linville Edom. We would have all our friends from Singers Glen with us. That was of no concern at the present time because we were on summer break. Then Daddy told us we were moving again. We moved on Monroe Street in Harrisonburg. *Oh no!* We were taking Aunt Meg with us. I had three friends there. One lived right beside us. One lived around the corner on Madison Street, and the other one around the next corner but still on Madison Street. The friend on the right and I used to walk around the block, singing as we went. The neighbors would go out on their porch to listen to us as we went by. They soon learned to know when we would be coming by their house. My other friend around the first corner on Madison Street always gave me treats from their freezer. I loved going to her house. We usually had Popsicles, Fudgsicles, and Imps. My other friend on Madison Street was a very pretty girl, and now Donnie was in puppy love. I left them alone because I knew what it was like to be in puppy love. I was still writing to my puppy love in Canada. To say the least, I knew how Donnie felt now. Good for good old Donnie. Emma would be going to Main Street School this year. Donnie and I were going to go to Linville Edom School because Daddy had arranged a ride for us with one of the teachers at Linville. Donnie was in his first year of high school, and eighth grade had just caught me. In high school, we had a different teacher for every class. There was a boy who sat behind me in my English class. He was always pestering me, like pulling my hair or unbuttoning my dress or blouse in the back. I wore those kinds of dresses at that time. I had just about all I could take from this guy, so I turned around and slapped his face really hard. As I said before, I had a lot of practice with Donnie. I packed a pretty good wallop, and the sound of it rang out all over the room. I looked at the teacher because I thought that I might be in big trouble, but she had a big, wide grin on her face. Then I knew I was safe. All my classmates were laughing. My science teacher was very different from my English teacher, and she wasn't putting up with any nonsense in her class. I really liked her even if she didn't put up with my shenanigans. There was a girl sitting in front of me who had long brown hair. I would put it up on her head and put pencils, pens, and anything else I could find in it. She didn't mind because she was getting a lot of attention from our classmates. They were all watching to see what was going to happen next. They all knew about my pranks. It wasn't long before they were about to find out. The teacher said, "Maxine, take her hair down this instant." I replied, "I had too much trouble getting it up there." All the kids were egging me on. The teacher put me in the corner next to the blackboard. That was a big mistake. I would turn around to see how my classmates were taking this. Some had settled down, but most of them were still egging me on. That was just enough to keep me going. The teacher was wearing a pretty red corduroy jumper with a white blouse. When she was where I wanted her to be, I blew chalk dust all over that pretty red jumper. I was in eighth grade now and should have been over all those pesky pranks, but I wasn't. Not yet anyhow. After class, the teacher kept me back to give me a good talking to. She said, "I hate to do this, but if you don't start behaving in class, I'm going to have to send you to the principal's office." I should have left it at that, but I just couldn't. I told her if she hated to send me to the principal's office, she didn't have to. That did it. I was off to the principal's office. The principal was very nice about it. He gave me a good talking to and told me I was going to have to start behaving in class. I told him I was sorry and promised to do better. I really tried to be good, but somehow, I just couldn't make the grade. My next encounter with the principal was when I skipped math class. I hated math. Here again, I didn't do it alone. I had to drag three of my friends with me. They didn't like math either, so it wasn't too hard to convince them that this was what we should do. We hid out in the girls' restroom. When math class started, the teacher realized there were four girls missing. They must have searched all over the place for us. Our dear old principal was pretty sharp. He thought we were probably in the girls' restroom. After all, where else could we hide? I told you, he was smart. He marched right in there and caught us. He took us all to his office, and being the wise man that he was, he didn't take us all in together. He took us one by one. He wanted to see what kind of excuses we would come up with. I don't know what the other girls told him, but when it came to me, he calmly asked why I skipped math class. I told him it was because I didn't like math and just didn't want to go to class. He looked like you could have knocked him over with a feather. By the look on his face, I knew he wasn't used to getting straight talk. He said, "That's a very honest answer. You may go."

CHAPTER TWENTY-EIGHT

There was a little creek near our house where Donnie trapped muskrats. Donnie and I were wading in the creek when Donnie challenged me to see who could dig in the mud the deepest. I started doing this with him until I felt the suction of the mud on my feet, and I got out. Donnie kept digging until he got so deep that he couldn't get out. I tried to pull him out, but the suction of the mud was hurting his feet, so I had to stop pulling. I asked him if he was trying to dig to China. He told me to just shut up and help him. I said, "A fine predicament you've got yourself into, brother." Then I stopped teasing him and ran up to the house to get Mom. I told her what a predicament Donnie had gotten into and how deep he was stuck in the mud. She got a shovel and shoveled him out, but it took some time to get him out. Once again, Mom saved the day.

CHAPTER TWENTY-NINE

$\mathcal{M}$oving time again! We bought a house at 455 East Elizabeth Street. Daddy was sick again. He was sick before we moved to Singers Glen the last time. I was in my second year of high school when he started getting sick again. I had a lot on me at that time with trying to keep up with my schoolwork, taking care of the house, and worrying about Daddy. I became so nervous that I would shake. Everybody began to notice. They took me to the doctor, and he told them to keep me home for a while. They did that, but I knew I was getting behind in my classes, and that made matters even worse. Daddy had gotten so sick he couldn't work anymore, so I quit school and went to work at the sewing factory where Mom worked. I did very well and was always bringing home extra money. I always made over my base, and when I did that, I could keep all over what I needed to make my base. At one time, I was running two machines at once. This was when my floor lady had to hold back my tickets so the price wouldn't be cut for the other girls. She gave them to me later when I wasn't making quite so much money. I was slowly getting over my nervousness. I liked working with Mom and being able to help her.

CHAPTER THIRTY

$\mathcal{T}$here was a girl living next door to us on Elizabeth Street. She was a very good friend. We called her Perky. Our houses were so close together. We could talk to each other from our bedroom windows. We rigged up a string reaching from my window to hers. It worked like a pulley. We sent notes back and fourth to each other after everyone else had gone to bed. She also had a younger brother who always mowed the lawn at their house, and I mowed at our house. Our property adjoined each other's, and this boy and I were always arguing about how far the property line ran. We never could agree on this, so we always had a little patch of grass running down the middle between our yards. He was just as stubborn as I was. We created our own property line.

There was another family who lived across the Street from us—They were the Linhoss family. There was Ray and Dot and they had three children. Kenny Linda and Charles. They also had a niece called Sandy. J. and I go to church with Sandy and her husband Emmette Mohler. Sandy is a beautiful lady inside and out. I love Sandy. She is a sweet sweet lady.

There was another family who lived on the corner up from the Linhoss family. They were the Wright family. There was Phillip and Audry and their two children Sandy and David. I was cutting Emma's hair and Audry liked it and asked me if I would cut Sandy's hair. I said "sure". I didn't know what I was doing—I just cut it. Soon more people on our street were sending their daughters for me to cut their hair. I was acquiring quite a little business for myself. I didn't charge any of them, but they always gave me a tip. Audry always gave me the biggest tip. She started treating me like a daughter. She was always inviting me to their house for meals and took me shopping and bought me beautiful clothes. I had never been treated this good in my life. She wouldn't let me pay for any of the clothes. I had money of my own from working at Sancar. Phillip was a detective and he was being transferred to Norton Virginia. Audry was really upset because she wanted to start me in cosmetology school. She asked Mom if she could adopt me. This was the second time somebody wanted to adopt me. I was at Audry's house when she called Mama on the phone. Mama didn't want to let me go and she and Audry had words over this. Audry told Mom she was working me too hard. Mom told her that it was the horse that pulled who got the beating. Audry said this horse was getting tired of getting the beating. I was only sixteen and Mom wouldn't let me go. Audry was going to visit her Mother in Louisville Kentucky and she asked Mom if I could go with them. Mom agreed to let me go. We went to Kentucky and I met her Mother Mrs. Ashbrook who was just as sweet as Audry. She welcomed me into her home and treated me just like David and Sandy. There was a sweet shop across the street from Mrs. Ashbrook's house and Audry gave all of us money to spend at the sweet shop. The next day we went to an amusement park. We rode all the rides they had including the Roller Coaster. David and Sandy were scared, but it was old hat to me because I had ridden a much bigger one in San Antonio Texas Where I went with a Lady and some friends of mine from church, but that is another story. We went to church with Mrs. Ashbrook on Sunday. Then it was time to go home where I would continue to work at Sancar and the Wright's would be moving to Norton Virginia. We kept in touch for a while.

There was another family who lived on Stuart Street right up from Elizabeth where we lived. This family was a very nice family. They had children and I would visit them from time to time. I was a people person. I met Pat. I remember Pat was trying to cut her hair. She wanted bangs, but she cut just a little too close to her scalp. They called me to see if I could fix it. I cut her bangs on farther back and pulled them up to cover what she had botched. We attend church now with Pat and her husband Rod. They have tour busses they run for people who like to take trips. This includes Me and J.

This was a very good area in Harrisonburg to live and I knew almost everybody. As I said I am a people person. Rochelle Cambbell and her husband Theron lived on up the hill from us. Rochelle and I have been friends for a very long time because we are both older than dirt. Rochelle also went to our church until she has been having health problems lately, but that all goes with being older than dirt. Another one of our friends is Evelyn

Washington who is also older than dirt. She attends the same church because we all know that God lives there and we are all looking forward to meeting Him soon. Sonny welcomes Him every Sunday. We are all a big happy family in the Lord. I have met so many wonderful people there. I can't begin to name them all unless I write another book.

CHAPTER THIRTY-ONE

$\mathcal{D}$addy wasn't doing well. He was sent back to Blue Ridge Sanatorium again. We would visit him on weekends when we were off work. He was getting very depressed, being alone in the hospital without the family, so I quit my job at the sewing factory and got a job at the sanatorium. I was still only sixteen. They really didn't hire people under eighteen, but Daddy talked to someone in charge about me and how good I was at everything I did, so they hired me. I was to prepare diabetic trays for people with diabetes who also had tuberculosis. I had to use substitutes and weigh everything. I prepared food for about a dozen people. I lived in the nurses' home with the nurses. They all took me under their wing. The nurses and I didn't go to work at the same time, so I had to walk up the hill from the nurses' home to the hospital with convicts who worked in the big kitchen, preparing food for the rest of the hospital. I was scared at first, but they had two guards walking with us, so that made me feel better. I continued substituting and weighing everything, and the patients' sugars started going down. The head doctor came up and was talking to the dietician. Then he came over to me. I was baking a diabetics' cake at that time. He just stayed there, watching me work. He was actually waiting for the cake to come out of the oven so he could sample it. He sampled it and told the dietician that was the best diabetics' cake he had ever tasted. He and the dietician went back over to her desk. They were in deep conversation about something. I knew it was something serious by the expression on their faces. I didn't know they were talking about me until the dietician told me the doctor wanted me to go to school to learn to be a dietician. I was thrilled to be given that opportunity. They had a teacher right there at the hospital. I was now going to school, working, and going to see Daddy in the evenings. Things were looking up for me. Not so for Daddy. He was going to have surgery to remove one lung and a lobe. Mom was moving the rest of the family to Charlottesville. She got a job in a pajama factory there. After she and the family moved over, I wanted to go home and live with them rather than stay at the nurses' home. We lived at 422 Virginia Avenue. It was a long way from there to the sanatorium, so the dietician went out of her way to pick me up in the morning and take me home in the evening. Everybody was so good to me. There was a nineteen-year-old boy there who was a patient. He was going to be released soon. Walter and I had finished with our puppy love at that time, so it was time to move on. It just so happened that Ed would be next in my life. Before he left the hospital, he proposed to me. We were supposed to get married after I finished school. I was home after work and on the weekends. Emma had gone down the street and found a bicycle they were selling for two dollars. Mom gave her the two dollars, and off she went to buy the bike. This old bike inspired me to write a poem about it. I wrote:

There is an old bike with one missing fender.
I'll take it to the fix-it shop and hope that they can
    mend her.
She wiggles, and she wobbles; she rattles, and she
    stalls.
The person who rides it is bound to get some falls.
The wheels are always spinning; you can hardly
    pull a hill.
I think it's better walking than to ride and have a
    spill.
The seat is on crooked, but that I never mind.
It goes down in the front and sticks up in behind.
I hope you'll take this warning, but just do as you
    like.
You are in for trouble when you buy a secondhand
    bike.

CHAPTER THIRTY-TWO

Again, Daddy got real sick, and the doctors decided to operate. I knew he had made peace with the Lord. I prayed and prayed for him. He was the same Daddy I knew as a child, and it seemed like he realized I really belonged to him in spite of looking like my half brother, Maynard. I felt the love he had for me as a child. The Lord had different plans for my daddy than I did. I was praying for him to recover again like before, but I know he had his chance for thirteen long years, and he didn't walk in obedience with God. I know our days are numbered, and when our number is up, we go to meet the Lord. I believe Daddy's number had been up thirteen years ago, but like Hezekiah, when he cried to God, he gave him fifteen more years. I believe he gave Daddy thirteen. The doctors took out one lung and a lobe. He lost fifteen pints of blood. Daddy was losing blood faster than they could pump it in. He died at the age of forty-nine. I was sixteen. Donnie was eighteen, Emma was ten, and Woodie was six. Mom was fifty when Daddy passed away, and she never remarried. This inspired me again to write a poem about Daddy. I wrote:

> My dad is sleeping so peacefully, and my heart is so sad and blue.
>
> And oh, how I miss his tender care and the laughter that I once knew.
>
> He's gone to mansions way up above, for his home now is in the sky.
>
> And I know some sweet day, I'll meet my dad, and I'll never have time to cry.
>
> Our friends have been so kind and good they gave us everything they could share.
>
> We thank them for their gifts, but nothing takes the place of my dad, who is resting way up there.
>
> So I'll go on my way, looking forward to that day when I can go to meet my dad.

CHAPTER THIRTY-THREE

After Daddy's death, we came home and went back to our home on Elizabeth Street. I was thankful that Mom kept the house and we had a place to come home to. Mom and I went back to work at Sancar. Again, I didn't finish what I started. It seemed this had become a pattern in my life, and I didn't like it. First, I didn't finish high school, and now I was giving up my big chance to become a dietician. We were on Elizabeth Street when I realized the thing with Ed was only puppy love. After all, I was experienced with puppy love. I wrote Ed my final letter and told him I was sorry, but I realized I wasn't in love with him. He had never given me a ring or anything. It was just an understanding between us. Shortly after I broke up with Ed, I met my future husband, Carroll "Buddy" Miller. Buddy wasn't a Christian, and I knew it. He didn't drink, but he smoked. This was my first big mistake. I was so madly in love with Buddy that I didn't think that far ahead to know there were consequences of marrying a man who wasn't a Christian. I was almost twenty when we got married, and Buddy was twenty-two. You would think we would have known what we were doing.

CHAPTER THIRTY-FOUR

$\mathscr{I}$ was still working at Sancar when I met my future husband, Carroll "Buddy" Miller. We dated for more than a year, and he asked me to marry him. We got married on August 2, 1957 at the preacher's house. The preacher, his wife, Buddy, and I were the only ones there. I was almost twenty when I got married. Buddy was twenty-two. We rented an apartment south of Harrisonburg, on the corner of Maryland Avenue and Main Street. This would be our home for the first year of our marriage. Then Buddy was drafted into the army. He was going to be stationed in Fort Hood, Texas. I was still working at the sewing factory and picking up Mom to take her to work with me. I was still helping Mom financially. Then Buddy called and wanted me to join him in Texas. He had a friend named Buck in the same unit. Buck had a wife named Ruth, who lived in Mount Jackson. I was to pick her up and take her with me to be with her husband. She didn't drive. There was a guy named Sam whom Buddy and I both knew. He was a country music singer who would help me drive if we stopped in Nashville, Tennessee, so he could make a demo. We all agreed to that, so I quit my job at Sancar, gave up my apartment to Buddy's sister Sue, and left all appliances and everything for her to use while we were gone. She would be paying the rent on the apartment. Then we were off to Texas. I was driving when we left. Sam sat in the middle of Ruth and me, with Sam's guitar in the backseat. Now I said, "Texas, here we come." Buddy had gotten a very small apartment in a little town called Coleen, Texas, right outside Fort Hood. Buck and Ruth stayed in the apartment with us and slept on a pullout sofa. Sam slept in the car since we didn't have room for him in the house. I drove Buddy to Fort Hood in the morning, and Sam would have to get out of the car so I could take Buddy to the base. Then he would go in our bed and sleep as long as he wanted to. Then I would take the car back to the apartment. We only had our car among the five of us. It was an old '52 Buick, which Buddy used when he worked for the city of Harrisonburg. One day, he took it to work and parked it close to where they were blasting. A big rock hit the car and caved the whole roof in. When Buddy came home, I looked out the window and saw the caved-in roof. I thought, how in the world did he have room enough to get in and drive home? But he managed to squeeze in. He pushed the roof up instead of in that evening so he could drive to work the next day. This was the same car I drove to Fort Hood, so you can imagine what kind of rag I was driving, but we were poor. We got poorer for about the next three weeks because we were supporting three extra people. After about three weeks, they all left, and Buddy and I were alone for the first time since I had gotten there. We went to the grocery store and stocked the freezer for the next two weeks. Then the refrigerator and the freezer went bad, and we didn't know it. That apartment was so run-down and smelly, we didn't even notice the smell of spoiled food. We had gotten used to the bad smell of the apartment. We didn't have a bathtub in the bathroom. We only had a shower and a stool. We didn't even have a sink in the bathroom. The apartment was too small for that. We had a sink in the kitchen, and that was it. I would go into the bathroom to take a shower and play with those little water bugs. It stayed damp there, and the water bugs were all over the place. I played with them and watch them curl up in a ball and roll across the floor. This was my entertainment. We didn't even have a television, but I had my water bugs. As I said, all our food spoiled, and it would be some time before Buddy got paid again. The only thing I could afford to eat was pancakes, and by this time, I learned I was pregnant. Buddy got lunch at the base, so he was doing pretty good, but I felt like I was starving all the time. He finally got another paycheck and took me out for a hamburger. That was the best hamburger I remember eating in my life. From that time on, I hated pancakes and still don't eat them.

CHAPTER THIRTY-FIVE

$\mathcal{B}$uddy was being sent to Germany. I was going to have to go back home. This time, I didn't have anybody to go with me. Buddy was trying to find somebody because he didn't want me to make that long trip by myself. He was trying to find somebody to keep me company and help me drive. He was getting desperate. As it turned out, we got neither. He finally found a guy whose wife lived in Elkton. I don't know how she got to Texas in the first place, because she was so bashful. Buddy and her husband brought her to meet me. She covered her face with her hands, and I couldn't even see what she looked like. Of course, she wouldn't be helping me drive, but she was all I had. I thought maybe she would warm up to me and at least keep me company on the way home. Not so. She didn't cover her face now, but she was far from being company for me. I was on my own, and I was determined I was going to get this girl home as fast as I could. Buddy had drawn a line on the map, showing the route I would be taking, and at that time, there wasn't the amount of traffic we have now. I drove for three days straight, stopping only long enough to catch a few winks, get gas, and pick up a few snacks for us. I got the keys to go to the bathroom, and then I gave the keys to her and told her to take them in and lay them on the counter in the station when she finished. We had gone for miles down the road when I looked over and saw she still had the keys in her hand. I found an address to mail the keys back, but not now. I was too intent on unloading my passenger. I would mail them after I got her home. We were getting closer. We were on the mountain at Chattanooga, Tennessee. It started to snow, and this was in April. I thought it would soon pass, but it seemed it was getting worse, and it was hard to see to drive. So I found a place to pull over, and that's exactly what I did. We stayed there until it started to get daylight, and then we started down the mountain. I had seen quite a few cars pass me on the mountain when I pulled over. Now I found those same cars in the ditch. I was thankful I chose to wait. I can look back now and see that God had his hand on me. He was always there when I needed him. When I was driving, I turned the radio up full blast to keep me awake. At times during the trip home, I had gotten so sleepy that when I saw the tail lights on the car ahead of me, I thought they were stop lights and I was going to another town. When we got to Roanoke, it was still snowing and it continued to snow, but I kept driving. It wasn't too bad, and my goal was to get this girl home. It was a good thing I got instructions from her husband where they lived. I finally got her home, and I can tell you, it wasn't too soon for me. After I got her home, I was on my way to Buddy's house. It was still snowing when I got back to Harrisonburg, and they were working on the bridge on Reservoir Street. I had been gone for some time and didn't know this construction was going on. I had to detour around the construction to get to Buddy's house, and the detour led me over a little cow path, or so it seemed to me, and the dirt was piled high on each side with no guardrails. To make matters worse, it was covered with snow. I had no choice. I had to take a shot at crossing this dangerous road. Here again, I believe the Lord had his hand on me because it was a very dangerous situation. I finally reached Buddy's house, and I remembered how happy his mom was to see me. I was safe now, so I unloaded my few belongings. The next thing I did was mail those keys back. Then I went back to work at Sancar. I had no trouble getting my job back. I was now trying to save for the baby.

CHAPTER THIRTY-SIX

$\mathcal{B}$efore the baby was born, Maynard got real sick, and they sent him to the Veterans Hospital in North Carolina. Mom wanted to go see him. By now, he had become an alcoholic. I told Mom I would take her because I also wanted to see Maynard. I was pretty sick myself with morning sickness. I ate ice all the way. The car started heating up before I could make it to the hospital. I knew I had to get this rag to a garage. I finally spotted a garage, but by then, the car was really hot, and steam was coming out of it. I thought it might catch fire. They knew what they were doing at that garage. They fixed the car, and we were on our way again. We got to the hospital fine. We asked for Maynard, and they took us in. He was in a very large room with beds on each side. Maynard was in one of the beds on the right side of the room. He didn't look good at all. He was all swollen, and his face was very red. We had a nice visit with him, but he told us that they were kicking him out of the navy on a dishonorable discharge, or he could get out on his own with an honorable discharge but there would be no pension. He didn't have a choice.

They were knocking him out of his pension either way. He had already served most of his twenty years in the navy. I thought this was very unfair since he had devoted most of his life in the navy. Maynard finally got well enough to go home to Elizabeth Street. He was very depressed and was drinking more than ever. Maynard was very likeable and found a bunch of his old drinking buddies who supplied him drinks. He had no money of his own. After I got Maynard settled in, I went back to Buddy's home, but I wasn't working at this time. I was too sick. I didn't want to be a burden on Buddy's mom, so I went back to Mom's and gave her my allotment check, which I got from Buddy, to help out until I could get back on my own.

CHAPTER THIRTY-SEVEN

$\mathcal{N}$ow there was Maynard, Emma, and me at the house. I was getting an allotment from Buddy for ninety dollars. Maynard used to help before he got sick, but there was no income except what I brought in my allotment. Before Gary was born, Mom had gone to West Virginia to see her mom and her sister. Grandma was living with Aunt Lizzy. I started having labor pains and called the doctor. He wanted me to get to the hospital right away. Then I called Donnie, and he and his wife took me to the hospital. Donnie called Mom and told her I had gone to the hospital. By the time she got there, Gary had already been born. I gave him his dad's middle name because I didn't like juniors. I named him Gary Layton Miller. Mom came in the next morning with a big vase of big yellow football mums. They were beautiful! After Gary was born, I went back to Mom's until he was older, at which time I got a job at a fruit stand on South Main Street where Donnie had a printing shop right beside the fruit stand. I rented a little apartment not far from there on South Main Street. I was still driving the old Buick. I paid $45 each month for rent, which took a lot of my allotment, and I still had to buy milk and baby food for Gary and gas for the car. I took Gary's secondhand playpen with me to work and kept him right with me while I worked to try to supplement my income. I had Gary with me at all times and didn't have to pay a babysitter. The money I made at the fruit stand wasn't much. I basically ate tomatoes and things I sold at the fruit stand. My boss said that was my fringe benefit since he wasn't paying me very much. I would put the playpen in the car and lock up the fruit stand in the evening. I had a small canvas car seat for Gary. Then we were ready to go home. He started out with just his bottle of Similac, but now I was starting to give him baby food and cereal. I would stuff Gary, but I wasn't eating much. I went down to ninety-seven pounds, but Gary was very healthy. I was thinner than I had ever been. That was OK because I had been battling the bulge most of my life. The Lord had his hand on me and carried me through the hard places. Donnie tried to help me by giving me a small job at his printing shop. He paid me a small salary, which helped out, but he wasn't making very much himself. Donnie and his wife, Sudie, did most of the work.

CHAPTER THIRTY-EIGHT

$\mathcal{I}$ worked at the fruit stand and was doing pretty good until Emma and her husband kept running in and out and causing trouble with my landlord, and I was asked to move. That ended my happy little home, which was so handy for me to get to the fruit stand and Donnie's printing shop. Now I was going to have to look for a place for me and Gary that I could afford. I looked all over, and I couldn't find a house I could afford, so I went to God about this and wrote a poem about it. I wrote:

Hast Thou Forsaken Me?

Sometimes my heart is burdened down with
    sorrow, and then I go to God on bended knee.
It seems as though I can't get through to heaven; I
    cry, "Oh, God, hast thou forsaken me?
Oh, Lord, you know how much I need an answer,
    so I am asking that you hear my plea.

And take away from me this heavy burden, and
    then I'll know you've not forsaken me."
Our Lord once felt alone and oh so weary, hanging
    on the cross in agony.
And just before he died, he softly whispered, "Oh,
    Father, why hast thou forsaken me?"
You sent your Son to die on that dark hillside to
    save us all from sin and set us free.
And when I think how much you really love me,
    then surely thou hast not forsaken me.

Buddy's mom was the answer to my prayer. She came to rescue me again and told me to go back and stay with them. She said they wouldn't charge me for any rent, and I could save my allotment for the time Buddy would be coming home. I only had a bed, Gary's high chair, his crib, a small table, and a couple of chairs. I managed to cram those into the old car and move back. The car may have looked bad, but you could get a lot of stuff in it. They were very good to me. I loved his mom. I didn't care much for his dad because he drank all the time and worried her. She was working and providing for the household. George and I locked horns on occasion, and I always spoke my mind. Evelyn, Buddy's sister, would come up from time to time, and this particular day, she was eating some fruit cocktail, and she started feeding Gary the juice. He really liked it and just lapped it up. Ebbie (Buddy's sister's nickname) was enjoying this. Later on, Ebbie worried that she might have made him sick, but my little boy was tough. It didn't bother him in the least.

CHAPTER THIRTY-NINE

While Buddy's mom was working, I would clean the house, wash dishes, etc. I was trying to show her in a very small way how much I appreciated her. She usually did the cooking. She loved to cook and made all kinds of delicious food. She was making me fat with all that good cooking, and Gary was beginning to eat from the table now. Buddy was discharged and was coming home. Gary was nine months old, and he had never seen him except in pictures I sent. I went to pick him up at an army base in New Jersey. I didn't know how to find him, so I went to the MP station. The police found him. I'm sure he was thinking, *What has she done now?* I just waited at the MP station until they located Buddy. Then we found a motel for the night. Our room also had a crib in it for Gary. He played with Gary awhile, and then I put Gary in the crib for the night. After Buddy and I had gone to bed, everything changed. Gary started crying. He was in a strange place and wasn't in his own crib at Grandma Miller's. He loved his grandma Miller. I tried to calm him down, but I just couldn't soothe him. Then Buddy jumped out of bed and grabbed Gary and whipped him very hard, which caused Gary to cry even more until he had the heaves. You can just imagine how furious I was. It was then I realized that Buddy wasn't the man I had married. I lit into him and gave him a real tongue-lashing. After I got Gary settled, I couldn't sleep the rest of the night. I refused to talk to Buddy. I didn't even talk to him when we got home. I was having flashbacks of the way my daddy used to beat me. My daddy physically abused me all those years, and I wasn't about to let that happen to Gary. I told Grandma Miller what had happened at the motel, and she had a hard time accepting what I told her because she had never seen him act that way. She told me that when Buddy was a child, he used to throw fits, but since then, he had been a mild-mannered boy. She was soon to find out for herself firsthand how he had changed. Her bedroom was upstairs on the left of the stairs, and our bedroom was next to hers. One night, Gary was crying again, and Buddy grabbed him out of his crib and started beating him again. I flew into Buddy, and we were getting loud. Grandma heard the ruckus and came over to see what was going on. She knew then that everything I told her was true. She was as furious as I was. She said, "Buddy, you don't beat a baby like that. You act as though he's a grown child who needs discipline. Gary doesn't even know why you are beating him." Grandma finally got Gary calmed down. She was so good with Gary. She was still upset with Buddy, and he knew it.

CHAPTER FORTY

$\mathcal{B}$uddy said it was time to move out of the homeplace and get a place of our own. He had saved some money while living at his home and working for the city of Harrisonburg. I had also saved my allotment money. We bought a shell home and were going to finish it ourselves. His mom had given each of her children an acre of land to build on that she had inherited from her mother. We all lived within walking distance of one another's place. We were going to build on the far end of the land, which used to be a cornfield. Things were very cold between Buddy and me. He was ignoring Gary altogether now. We started moving in when it was only a shell and rafters. The Tobins lived right in front of us, with only a small lane separating the property. The Boones lived farther up that lane. Up the lane from the Boones lived the Smallwoods. Mel Smallwood couldn't talk plain, and he also had a drinking problem. He did some carpentry work. He didn't work very much, but he helped us when he wasn't too drunk to work. Before we got the house, we put a full basement under it, and Mel was doing the work. There was a long span on each wall, about sixty feet. I said, "Buddy, don't you think we should brace that wall?" He said no; he and Mel knew what they were doing. I dropped the subject because after all, I didn't know anything about building a house.

CHAPTER FORTY-ONE

$\mathcal{W}$e only paid $6,000 for the shell and broke it down in payments. Our payments were very low. We had the subfloor in the big room, which would later become our living room. Buddy and I started putting up Sheetrock. Buddy drove the nails, and I held up the Sheetrock with the help of a two-by-four. It was still heavy to begin with for my five-foot, one-hundred-pound frame, but I was tough. I had done plenty of hard work in my life. I was tougher now than I had ever been. With every nail that Buddy drove in, the lighter my job became, until at the end it was a piece of cake. We were putting up four-by-eight sheets. Gary had a little workbench I had bought for him, and I thought he was working on his workbench while Buddy and I put up Sheetrock. We had our TV in that room where Gary liked to watch cartoons. I looked around to see what Gary was doing. He wasn't working on his workbench. He was driving Sheetrock nails in the speaker of the TV. The speaker was on the left side, with little square holes covered with cloth. We turned on the TV, and it wouldn't come on, but if you tapped one of the tubes with the screwdriver, it would come on for a while and then go back off. It would come back on when you tapped it again, so Gary got the hang of this pretty quick. When he was watching his cartoons and the set went off, he would say, "Mommy, get the dedibie." That meant *screwdriver*.

CHAPTER FORTY-TWO

$\mathcal{B}$uddy hired Mel to move the job along a little faster. Since he had a man helping him instead of a puny, little woman, I became their gofer—go for this and go for that. Now we had the ceiling, walls, and subfloor in the big room. Things were going pretty good at this time, and Buddy had stopped whipping Gary before we left the homeplace. He knew he would have a confrontation with me if he kept that up, and he didn't like that one little bit. Mel would come down from time to time and help with more of the other rooms. We had two-by-fours stashed in our unfinished basement. Mel would say "Maie," meaning Macky—that's what Mel called me—"bring me a two a tor," meaning *two-by-four*. He had a girlfriend, who lived with him, and I asked him what she was doing. He said, "Her up there in the rain barrel." I said, "What is she doing in the rain barrel?" He said, "Toten," meaning *floating*. Old Mel was quite a character but very likeable. I could always tell when he was coming to the house because he would yell "Hey, hey" before he ever got there. I would say, "Mel, you're drunk, just keep going." He would just laugh and go on down the road. He would be down on the main road, flagging traffic until the police would go by and lock him up for the night. He reminded me of Otis, the old drunk on the *Andy Griffith Show*. He only stayed in jail one night, but it wasn't long before he was out flagging traffic and going back to jail.

CHAPTER FORTY-THREE

$\mathcal{G}$ary also liked those little golden books, which I would read to him each night. We bought one every time we went to the grocery store. They always had animal stories and a lot of cute stories in them. I was reading to him about a squirrel. He said, "Mommy, draw that squirrel for me." I told him I couldn't draw anything. I could never draw in school. Gary kept insisting that I draw that squirrel, so to please him, I got a pencil and a piece of paper and looked at the book and tried to follow the lines of the squirrel. To my amazement, the squirrel I had drawn looked just like the one in the book. Then I thought that if I could enlarge those little characters, I could draw them on his walls in his room. I was able to enlarge them, so I picked up some colored pencils at the store and proceeded to color the characters I had drawn. This was all done with those little colored pencils. We were dirt poor, and I couldn't afford to buy paint. I drew Dumbo the elephant, the seven-hump Wump, a crow with a cigar in his mouth, a mouse with a pea in his mouth, Cutie Bear, and Peter Rabbit and all his family. The neighbors would come to the house just to see

Gary's room. Then I started drawing faces on his belly with the mouth at his navel. When he worked his belly, the little character looked like it was talking. Gary had to go show all the kids in the neighborhood his belly. Then all those kids came to me to draw faces on them. We may have been poor, but we had fun. I enjoyed just watching the kids have a good time.

CHAPTER FORTY-FOUR

$\mathscr{B}$efore we built our house, Buddy asked Peck Tobin if we could have a right-of-way over their property. Buddy had known Peck for years. Peck said, "Sure, Bud." There was a hollow in the lane, which flooded every time it rained. Buddy thought he would show his appreciation for Peck letting us use the lane, so he put in a large culvert so the water could run through. Before Buddy put the culvert in, the lane flooded every time it rained, and at times, the Tobins couldn't get in or out. We used the lane for some time. Then one day, Eva came up and told Buddy she didn't want us to use it anymore. Buddy had nothing in writing; he just took Peck at his word. Buddy kept using it anyhow because he had to go to work and had no other way out. There was a bank between our yard and their lane. Buddy would take it slow and easy when he crossed over. Eva got real upset because Buddy kept using the lane, so she sent her youngest son up during the night to set up a booby trap. He put all kinds of junk on the other side of the bank that Buddy was unable to see when he crossed over. It tore our car all to pieces, and he couldn't go to work that day. Little could we afford this because now we would have to buy another car, and we still didn't have a right-of-way out. Somehow, we managed to buy another car and make payments on it. We finally got rid of the rag but only because we were forced to get rid of it because it was totaled by the booby trap.

CHAPTER FORTY-FIVE

When Gary was four and Sabrina (Emma's daughter) was two, Emma brought Sabrina to my house and asked me to take care of her for a little while, and she would be back that evening to pick her up. She didn't come back that day, and she didn't bring any clean clothes for Sabrina or milk for her bottle or anything. When she brought her, she had a bottle of sour milk. I had some milk on hand at that time, but I knew if she didn't come back, I would have to get more milk and clothes. When she brought her, she needed her diaper changed, and she had one of her old tops on Sabrina, so she really didn't have any clothes of her own. I had diapers left from Gary, so I used those and washed them. We didn't have disposable diapers. Sue (Buddy's sister) had a daughter a little older than Sabrina, so she let me have some clothes for Sabrina. The next day came and still no Emma. After a week went by, I thought she wasn't coming back, so I just took Sabrina in the family as though she always belonged there. She and Gary were like brother and sister and still are to this day. Sabrina was my niece, but she seemed more like a daughter, so I started calling her my daughter-niece. We are still very close. She became more and more a part of the family, and her great-grandfather found out where she was, so he would bring her her milk, toys, etc. The second week went by and still no Emma, but I always had a cloud hanging over my head, thinking she would come and take Sabrina away from me. At the end of the third week, Emma finally showed up, demanding to take her. Of course, I didn't want to let her go. Emma had been sleeping in a car with her boyfriend, and I knew that was no place for Sabrina, but I just couldn't reason with her. I was holding Sabrina in my arms when she grabbed both of my arms, and when she did, I dropped Sabrina. I saw she wasn't hurt, and I lit into Emma. We went round and round, but she took Sabrina. She was her mother regardless if she was a sorry one. To this day, Sabrina is sorry she didn't get to stay with me and grow up with Gary, but both Gary and I have stayed very close to Sabrina all these years.

CHAPTER FORTY-SIX

Gary and I were in the house when a big storm came up. It rained and rained. Suddenly, I heard a loud crash. It shook the whole house. I grabbed Gary and got out of there as fast as I could. I thought the whole house was going to go. I ran to the next-door neighbor's house. After the rain subsided, I looked up at the house, and it was still standing. I thought, "Thank God for that!" I went up to the house to see what had caused the big crash. I walked to the back where the sixty-foot wall was. Now that wall was completely gone. I remembered when I told Buddy to brace it, he said he and Mel knew what they were doing. Now we had a big mess to clean up besides having to replace the wall. Buddy not only got somebody who knew what they were doing to replace the wall, but he also made sure they braced it. I felt like telling him "Told you so," but I bit my tongue and didn't say anything. I'm sure he knew what I was thinking.

CHAPTER FORTY-SEVEN

$\mathcal{I}$ got a part-time job at a little Laundromat in the Clover Leaf Shopping Center. I was looking for a job where I could take Gary with me, and this fit the bill. Gary kept himself occupied by finding change in the dryers. He also helped me tidy up the place. He enjoyed going to work with me. This worked out very well, but I needed to make a little more money for Gary's Christmas, so I went back to work during the Christmas rush at Sancar. I got Buddy's sister, Sue, to watch Gary during that time. I told them at Sancar I would only be working during the Christmas rush. They took me on those terms. After the Christmas rush, I went back to my part-time job at the laundry. This was enough to buy gas for the car and have a little extra to do things with Gary. I didn't want to leave him very much because I didn't want to lose out on watching him grow up.

CHAPTER FORTY-EIGHT

$\mathcal{B}$uddy continued to do his own thing, like meeting some of his friends at Drug Fair, but we still didn't do anything as a family. On weekends, Buddy usually watched football games or went fishing with his brother-in-law. Gary was in his room, playing, and Buddy was watching football. I felt alone and somewhat depressed when I wrote another poem. I wrote about the good old days. I wrote:

> When family and friends got together and the kids
>   went out to play,
> There was time for conversation, and that's how I
>   wish it could stay.
> But times have changed and friends have too, and
>   the kids have gone astray.
> They have minds of their own, no respect for the
>   home, and their manners have gone away.
> They butt in on the conversation and throw
>   tantrums because they know.

Instead of correcting their children, they will just
    have to go.
This kind of behavior goes on now with the kids
    that modern folks raise.
They've forgotten the strap and the woodshed
That were used in the good old days.
Then TV came into the household. That monster
    took over the home.
If football games are not your thing, you spend
    your time alone.
What happened to family discussions and caring
    for one and all?
It's all gone away with that very last play as the
    runner ran off with the ball.
You try your best to be patient until a commercial
    comes on,
But by that time, your thought in mind has been
    there, come and gone.
I guess it's best to forget it, as you think of your
    childhood ways.
What was before simply is no more, as it was in
    the good old days.

CHAPTER FORTY-NINE

$\mathcal{B}$uddy was ignoring Gary altogether now. He acted as though Gary didn't exist, so I became both father and mother to Gary. I played games with him. We played ball and badminton and anything else we could come up with. We played badminton over the clothesline in our backyard. We really got quite good at hitting that little birdie. This became our favorite game. All this didn't take the place of Buddy's neglect. Gary would watch his cousins go hunting and fishing with their dads, and Gary was the only boy left at home. He would beg his dad to let him go, but Buddy would refuse every time. Buddy told him he would take him when he was six years old. I bought Gary a small rod and reel, anticipating the time Gary would turn six. He would take his little rod and reel and practice casting in his plastic swimming pool. When Gary turned six, he reminded Buddy of his promise. Of course, Buddy only told him that to get him off his back. Buddy and his friend left to go fishing. They had bought a boat together. Gary started crying because not only was he disappointed because he couldn't go fishing again but also because his dad had lied to him. This just broke my heart. I said, "Honey, stop crying. Mama will take you fishing." I didn't know the first thing about fishing. I had never gone fishing. I knew they would dig worms for bait. I had also heard that some of them used canned whole corn kernel. I put a tub in the trunk and filled it with ice. It was one of those half tubs. Gary got his rod and reel. I didn't want to mess with those dirty old worms, so I took a can of corn for bait. We jumped in the car, and we were headed to find a fishing hole. Gary was so excited. I told him to watch for a fishing hole while I drove. We went out West Market Street and to Rawley Springs. I thought we might find a fishing hole there, but all we saw were people swimming. There was probably a fishing hole there somewhere, but since we couldn't see it from the road, I just kept driving. We came to the West Virginia line. I kept driving, and Gary saw a bunch of people at a big body of water. It was much bigger than any plain old fishing hole we had seen. We thought this would be a good place, so I drove in. We passed some little shacks on our way in. We got to the fishing hole, and Gary baited his hook with corn. He threw his line in the water. It had no more than hit the water when he was catching fish. He was having the time of his young life. I would throw the fish in the tub. We had that tub full of fish. Gary was ecstatic. I told him our tub was full so we better go home now. All good things must come to an end. We got back in the car and were on our way home. We both felt real good about our first day of fishing. I told Gary, "I bet you caught more fish than your daddy and his friend put together." We had so many fish that I told Gary we would stop by Grandma Roadcap's house and share some with her. We would still have enough for Grandma Miller and ourselves. Mom was still living on Elizabeth Street; and Maynard, my half brother, was there. We got them to come out to the car to see what we had in the trunk. Maynard said, "Where did you catch all those fish?" I said, "Somewhere in West Virginia." I really didn't know exactly where we were. Maynard said, "Did you pay for them?" I said, "No, why?" He said he thought I was supposed to pay for them. I said, "I didn't see anybody to pay, and I didn't know I was supposed to pay for them." He told me I was supposed to have them weighed, and they would tell me how much I owed. I never knew of Buddy and the guys ever paying for fish they caught. Maynard was really giving me the third degree. After all, I only took Gary fishing. Maynard said he thought I got them at a hatchery. I didn't even know what a hatchery was. I thought they just had babies in the water they were in. Maynard said, "Maxine, you stole those fish!" I felt really badly about this. I said, "I'll just take them back." He said, "Do you want to cause those people to lose their jobs?" I said, "No, of course not. Why would I cause them to lose their jobs?" He said, "If you take them back, the people who let you through without paying would probably lose their jobs." That made me feel even worse. Somehow, I seemed to be in trouble no matter what I tried to do. I was only taking my son fishing and trying to make up for his disappointment of not being allowed to go with his daddy. Big deal! He said that about all I could do without causing more problems was to just keep the fish. I took his advice and kept the fish. I sure learned a lot about fishing in a very short time. I shared the fish with them. I thought that was the least I could do since that was the reason I was there in the first place. If I hadn't stopped to share the fish with Mom and Maynard, I wouldn't have known I did anything wrong. Now I was ridden with guilt. I was trying to tell Buddy what I had done, but as usual, he didn't take the time to listen to me. I prayed that God would forgive me because I knew it was a sin to steal.

CHAPTER FIFTY

$\mathcal{I}$ had a little lamb I raised in Gary's playpen. She wasn't very healthy when I got her. I would get up in the night and feed my lamb just like I would feed a baby. The lamb started getting too big for the playpen, so Buddy built her a little house in the backyard, with a fence around it so we could keep her in a little area and I could feed her through the fence. Buddy liked Lamb Chops and was very proud of the way she had grown from the unhealthy lamb she was when I got her. Gary loved Lamb Chops as much as I did. He was an animal lover. He was always bringing something home for me to nurse back to health if at all possible, and most of the time, it was a success. After Eva closed our right-of-way after Peck had promised Buddy we could use it, we had to make other arrangements so Buddy could go to work. The only other possible way out was to go over Bobby and Evelyn's property. Bobby Smith was Buddy's sister's husband. There was only a small path there at that time, but Buddy could get enough traction to take it slow and easy and get to the end of the lane. He would park the car there and walk to the house so he could go to work the next morning. Bobby Smith made Buddy an offer, which I strongly disagreed with. He offered to give us a right-of-way over his property if I would give him my Lamb Chops. They all knew how much I loved that lamb. I was very upset about this and thought it was so unfair to even ask for my lamb. Bobby promised if I would give him my lamb, he would never sell her. At this time, she had become a beautiful sheep. He told me I could see her anytime I wanted to. I was still very reluctant, but I thought if I could see her all the time, it wouldn't make much difference. Since Bobby promised not to sell her, I thought it would be OK, and it would make it easier for Buddy to get to work. Even after Buddy got to the main lane in front of Bobby Smith's house, the lane was so rough. I renamed it the Buffalo Trail. After a hard rain, the lane would get so bad, we would all get together to fill it in with rocks. We could throw in big rocks, and they would quickly disappear. We got the road in shape so we could travel on it, and the little path became a lane.

I know it wasn't more than three weeks before Bobby sold my sheep. My heart was broken again. I just took people at their word much too much. She was such a beautiful sheep, and a lot of people wanted to buy her from us, but I never would sell her no matter how much they offered me. She just meant so much to me to sell her, but I thought the arrangement with Bobby Smith wouldn't be final. Now I knew I would never see my baby again. I couldn't eat or sleep for a long time after that, but I slowly began to accept it and go on with my life. But I never got over what Bobby Smith did to me, and I never felt the same about him after that. I felt the same way about the Tobins. I just found it so hard to believe people could so easily break their promises. Their word meant absolutely nothing. I didn't hold a grudge, and I still took Eva to town when she needed to go because she didn't drive. I also treated Bobby nicely, but I never trusted them again. I never forgot what I heard Fred Price say on his TV program. He said, "If you go into your neighbor's yard who has a dog and the dog bites you, don't go back in that neighbor's yard." I really liked watching that preacher when I was between churches for one reason or another. Mom watched him too because when I wasn't in church, neither was she. She loved to go to church, and she read her Bible every day and really lived the Christian life. She also prayed for everybody every day and prayed for God to forgive her of any sins she had committed that she was unaware of. Not only was she my mother, whom I adored, but she was also a good, honest person. I guess that is where I learned to trust people.

I wrote a poem concerning all I had to be thankful for in spite of all the disappointments I had received from my neighbors and in-laws. I wrote:

> Lord, I've been so busy lately that I just about forgot to thank you for my blessings, and Lord, they're quite a lot.

> For the very air we breathe, Lord, each breath from you we borrow, without your love and mercy, for us there's no tomorrow.

> Right now I want to tell you that I'm sorry I forgot to thank you for my husband and that precious little tot

For a mother I love dearly, who could ask for any more? For home and food and comforts and the loved ones I adore.

These things we take for granted, the sunshine and the rain, our health and our happiness, I thank you once again.

I hope that you'll forgive me. Of course, I know you will; in spite of all my faults, Lord, I know you love me still.

CHAPTER FIFTY-ONE

$\mathcal{G}$ary continued to bring in unhealthy animals. This time, it was two pigs. We called them Red and Seamore. They got to be so tame they were more like puppies than pigs. I had a little Pekingese dog, and the pigs and the dog played together. Speaking of my dog, she was something else I dearly loved. As I got older, it seemed like I got more attached to my animals; and if anything happened to them, I was crushed, but I still couldn't turn away anything I could help. My Pekingese was registered. Her mother's name was Trixie of York, and her father was Bandy Jo. Gary liked the name of Maidy, and I liked the name Misty, so we compromised and called her Wee Misty Maiden, but she always went by the name Misty. She was such a sweet little thing most of the time, but if she thought anybody was doing something to me, she went after them. She used to ride on my left leg when we went for a ride and I was driving. She would stand on her hind legs and beg for jerky. She only lived six years. I took her to the animal hospital, and they did everything they knew to do for her, but they couldn't save her. Here again, I was heartbroken and wound up in bed for three days. To top it all off, Buddy said we were going to butcher the pigs. He said that was what they were for. I didn't think that was what they were for. They were my pets. It seemed that anything I got that I really loved, I lost. First, if you recall, it was my goat, Billy, then Lamb Chops and my pigs, and now my very precious Misty was gone. I have never gotten another dog since then. Gary was still bringing in animals, but most of them were healthy. At one time, he had twenty-five teddy bear hamsters, which ran around his room in a tube called a Habitrail, and they had little wheels to play on and houses to get into when they wanted their privacy. If you cleaned their cages and moved them a little out of their spot, they would put it back the way they had it before. They were smart little critters. We went to Glen's Fair Price Store and bought a long-haired guinea pig. Gary thought we were going to have to take her to the vet to see why she was so swollen. We found out overnight. She had two little ones. We thought we were buying one, but we wound up with three.

CHAPTER FIFTY-TWO

$\mathcal{I}$ had been taking Gary to the little chapel up the road from our house. It was called Mabel Memorial Chapel. Buddy wouldn't go, but he didn't object to us going. I also picked up Mom and took her to the little chapel. After a while, they asked me to teach Sunday school at the chapel. I taught the primary class, which included Gary. We would read the lesson, discuss what we had read, and have our prayer. Then I would do a little craft with them. My friend Jo also liked to do crafts, so she helped with all of them. Gary got sprinkled in that little chapel. Although I liked going to the chapel, I didn't get much out of the sermons. They were just dry.

CHAPTER FIFTY-THREE

$\mathcal{G}$ary and I hadn't been out for a drive for some time, and we both needed to get out of the house. I also knew if I went very far, Buddy would be checking my mileage to see how far I had gone. There was this old man who pumped gas for me all the time. I had to get gas, so I asked him if he could disconnect my speedometer cable. I had known him for years and he knew my situation, so he said he would do it for me. I told him we just needed to get out of the house for a while, and I would stop by on my way back to get him to hook it back up again. He agreed to do that, so Gary and I were off to somewhere. I really didn't know where at that time. I started driving north on 81. We got to New Market, but we didn't see anything of real interest there, so I started up the mountain toward Luray. It was beautiful up there. We saw a little path, which we thought was probably a walking trail, so we decided to walk this trail to see what we could see. I was sure we would see some pretty birds and maybe a squirrel or a rabbit. I couldn't imagine what we actually saw. We saw this beautiful big pheasant. Gary was so excited about seeing such a beautiful bird. This was more than just the pretty birds I thought we might see. I told him not to tell his daddy where we had been. Gary was chattering about the pheasant all the way back to the station. The old man hooked my cable up again, and we were on our way home. When Buddy came home, Gary blurted out about the pheasant because he was so excited about it. Buddy said, "Where did you see a pheasant?" I had to think fast. I surely couldn't tell him up on Luray Mountain. I just couldn't! So I made up a story. I told him it was in that field across from Mabel Memorial Chapel. There was a big field across from the church. I knew it had to be somewhere close to home, so that was my story, and I was sticking to it. That evening, Buddy went over to his brother-in-law's house. He always hunted with him. He told him what we had seen and where we saw it. Later that same evening, his brother-in-law came over, carrying this pheasant, and he told Buddy, "It was exactly where she said it was." It was all Gary and I could do to keep our composure. Nobody could have been more surprised than we were! We both knew it was just a made-up story. My story became the truth, but I had no idea it would turn out that way, so I was still guilty of making up the story. I had to ask God to forgive me for that. I was always asking forgiveness for something. I was always doing something I shouldn't have done.

CHAPTER FIFTY-FOUR

$\mathcal{G}$ary's grandpa Miller died when Gary was eleven years old. It was close to Halloween. Gary had some candy corn in each side of his mouth when the Undertaker came. When the Undertaker walked in, Gary said, "All I vant is your blood." The Undertaker said, "You are quite a character." Everybody got a good laugh and loosened up a little bit. Grandma Miller never remarried. She had a pretty rough life with George, and I guess she didn't want to try it again. She was only fifty when he died. She continued to work at her job and bake pies for people. Everybody loved her homemade pies. She was always doing something for somebody, and all she wanted was a little appreciation. She sure didn't get any from George. She also kept busy in the summer with her flower and vegetable gardens. She was always in a good mood, except maybe when George got on her nerves with his drinking. She used to come over to visit, and I always looked forward to seeing her. She may have been alone, but she wasn't lonely. She had her family all around her. We used to take her and Mom to PTL when we went. Gary had an old Dodge van he had fixed up for camping. It had a bed in it, so she and Mom slept most of the way there. They both enjoyed that trip.

CHAPTER FIFTY-FIVE

$\mathcal{I}$ quit going to the chapel and started going to a church called Ray of Hope. I could certainly use a ray of hope about now. We attended the church and were enjoying it very much. I would pick up Mom on Sunday and take her with me. When anybody mentioned church, she was always ready to go. She didn't drive, so if there was no one to pick her up, she just had to stay home. She had no other choice. As we got into the church, we formed a little trio. It was me and Gary and the preacher's daughter. We called the trio the Maranatha Trio. The preacher's daughter played the guitar. She also taught Gary to play the guitar. Her daddy called us the Hillbillies. He also sang in a quartet. I was sewing dresses for the women in the quartet and making ties for the men to match the women's dresses. The pastor would hold revivals sometimes at different churches. Our trio went with him. We were in Petersburg, Virginia, and we were singing "Cross Over the River." Some of the lyrics were "I haven't crossed it yet, but my feet are already wet." A lady in the congregation was always requesting "the foot wet song." After the revival was over,

I started babysitting for my neighbor. The baby was a girl. They called her Cindy, but I called her Cokie. She wasn't but about two weeks old when Brenda, her mother, went back to work. Her mother worked long hours, and she was usually late picking her up in the evening. She was with me more than she was with her mother, so she started calling me Mom from the time she could talk. She seemed like my daughter, and a lot of people thought she was my daughter. She started staying with me more and more. She didn't want to go home, so I was also keeping her on weekends. I wanted to take her to church with me on Sundays, but they mostly dressed her in pants. I started making her dresses to wear to church. She became a part of our family. I sent her to school from my house. When she started first grade, her mom got her all registered, and after she thought she was settled, she went back to work. She wasn't really settled because she started crying and said she wanted her mama. The school called Brenda, and she went back to the school. When she got there, Cokie told the teacher, "Not that mama. I want my other mama." I'm sure this really embarrassed Brenda. They couldn't get Cokie to calm down, so Brenda called me and asked me if I would go to the school. Of course, I went. When Cokie saw me, she was happy. I consoled her for a while and told her I was the same way when I started first grade. I cried for Mama too, and they sent Donnie to be with me the first day. I told Cokie, "After the first day, I didn't need Donnie anymore because I was a big girl going to school, and you are a big girl going to school. I'll be home in the evening when you come home." She accepted that, and I went home. I was there for her when she came home, and she did fine after the first day. We continued to go to the same church, and I always took Cokie with me. We also had a bus to take people to church when they didn't have a ride. I was feeling real good about my spiritual life there. We went there for many years. Then Buddy told me that if I would go back to the chapel, he would start going to church with us. I agreed to do that if it would get him in church. Mom and I hated to leave Ray of Hope, but I went back to the chapel. Mom went with us. I had always picked her up the first time. Buddy started going with us. The attendance at the chapel was very small, so I decided to form a singing group there that would include Buddy. He had a good singing voice. We had three guys singing the lead part, and Gary and I sang harmony. We were known as the Chapel Five. We would go each week to one of the group's houses to practice for Sunday morning. We went to a different house each week. We had a good time just with practice and fellowship. We also had snacks of some kind. There always have to be snacks. This lasted for a couple of years until Buddy and Gary dropped out. That left only three of us and only me singing harmony. It was good while it lasted.

CHAPTER FIFTY-SIX

$\mathcal{I}$ had been watching Fred Price on television, and I liked him very much. There was a church near Dayton called Word Ministries, so I thought I would go and see if it had some life. Mom always went with me. Sometimes, Gary would go. We started attending, and we were getting food for our soul again. They asked me to teach Sunday school there, so I taught about the same age of children as I did at the chapel. I also did crafts with them with Bible verses on the craft. A friend and I also did a puppet show for the kids. I made the puppets. The church was growing by leaps and bounds. We started building a new church.

Buddy got very sick. He had turned yellow with jaundice. We took him to the hospital to get him checked out. They ran all kinds of tests on him and couldn't find anything that could be causing the jaundice. Then he was diagnosed with pancreatic cancer. He had to have surgery. I knew he had to make things right with the Lord, but I knew I couldn't force it. He had to accept Jesus on his own. I would talk to him about attending church with me. He finally told me he would go. He really enjoyed it. He gave his heart to the Lord there and continued to attend that church. He had surgery in April. He came through the surgery fine. I asked the doctor if he got it all. He told me he got all he could see. That didn't tell me much, and I didn't realize how very serious pancreatic cancer was. He was taking radiation after surgery, and he seemed to be doing very well. By July, he was running a fever that we couldn't get down. There was nothing to do but take him to the hospital. Immediately after we got there, they put him on ice, which brought his temperature down; but the next morning, he had a stroke. This blinded him in the left eye, and he couldn't speak. He could understand but couldn't speak. I could tell what he needed most of the time. I stayed in the room with him day and night and slept in a recliner. His mom would come every now and then and let me go home for a while to get some very much needed rest. She was always there to help when you needed her, but she was getting up in years by now, and I didn't want her to get too tired out. They told me I could probably just take him home since they couldn't do any more for him. I got a hospital bed for him and had it delivered to our house. He was on a feeding tube, and I had to learn how to clean that, and I also learned how to give him shots. I was all set now to take him home. The family was looking forward to him coming home, but he passed away before I had a chance to get him home. Just before he died, they told me if there was anything I wanted to say to him to say it now because he wouldn't be there much longer. I told him he was going to be with Jesus, and I would soon be there too. He took his last breath, and he was gone. He died on September 5, 1989. We had been married thirty-two years. Gary had moved out years ago, so I would be by myself for the first time. Gary moved back with me later on. I was doing a lot of craftwork at that time. In fact, I had been doing crafts for many years before Buddy died. I put them in craft shops all around the area, and they would get a percentage from all sales. After Buddy died, I got into crafts more than ever. I thought I would be like Mom and Buddy's mom and just throw myself into more work. This seemed to be going very well, but the Lord had different plans for me.

CHAPTER FIFTY-SEVEN

$\mathcal{I}$ had known J. Holsinger since we were in our teens, but I
hadn't seen him for a long time. One day, I was out shopping and
ran into his best friend Jim. During our conversation, I told him
Buddy had passed away. Since J was single again, Jim told him
he had run into me and about what had happened in my life. J
called me and asked me to go to dinner with him. I told him I
was just too busy. I pictured him being bald and fat and talked
myself out of getting involved with anybody. He didn't give up.
He must have called me three times or more, and I was always
busy, but this time he said, "I only want to take you to dinner." I
thought that since he put it that way, maybe I'll just go to dinner
without really getting involved with him, so I finally accepted the
invitation. He drove up in his Nissan 300 ZX. He was wearing
a red-and-white checked shirt, which matched his car. I was
impressed, to say the least! He wasn't bald and fat either—far
from it. He had a head full of hair, and he was thin. He took me
to my favorite place for dinner, which was the Bar-B-Que Ranch.
We both went there all the time when we were young. We sat and

talked about old times, and I realized that he was very nice. We dated regularly after that, and he asked me to marry him. By this time, I was certain that he was the one for me; and although I didn't really want to get married again, I knew the Lord was working for my good. I told J I would marry him under one condition, and that was that he would attend church with me. I wasn't going to make the same mistake with him as I did with Buddy. J hadn't been attending church on a regular basis at that time, but he agreed to go with me. He started going with me even while we were still dating. On Valentine's Day in 1991, we were married. We got married at my home with just a few friends and both our moms. J was forty-nine, and I was fifty-three. I often tease him about marrying an old woman. J had been married twice, and neither one had worked out. I told him he had to try three times to get it right. J, Mom, and I were still attending Word Ministries. J was enjoying going to the church. He had been going to dry churches before that, and he was glad he found a church with some life. I continued to teach Sunday school, and Mom and J listened to the sermon. I had the sermon on tape even though I wasn't in the church service.

CHAPTER FIFTY-EIGHT

*U*nlike my first marriage, J loved to travel, and he never restricted me from going anywhere I wanted to go, like shopping, etc. I would take one day each week and take Mom wherever she wanted to go. I called this Mom's Day Out. When J and I first got married, I moved to Broadway. He was living in a double-wide mobile home at that time, which was very nice. J and I lived in the double-wide for the next four years. Gary had come home and was living in the house in Harrisonburg. He and his grandma Miller were very close. He helped her whenever she needed help with anything.

J and I left for a trip to New Mexico, where he wanted to visit one of his old air force buddies. He hadn't seen him in years and had a lot of catching up to do. His wife and I visited and got to know each other. They wanted us to spend the night with them, so we spent the night, but early the next morning, we were off again to visit friends in Louisiana, where J was stationed when he was in the air force at England Air Force Base. I met Jim and

Bettie. They were very nice people, and I liked them very much. Of course, J had known them years ago when he was in service. They had a lot of nurseries right near their house, and I loved going through those nurseries. I bought some seedlings, and they were shipping them to me at home. Among my many seedlings, I bought two bald cypresses. Those seedlings are beautiful big trees now. I don't see anything like them in this area. We went to dinner with Jim and Bettie, and then they wanted us to spend the night with them. We spent that night with Jim and Bettie. The next day, we were on our way again. This time, we visited Don and Madge Odom. Madge was a girl from Broadway, and J grew up with her, but I didn't know her. J's mom and Madge's mom were best friends. When I met Madge and Don, they were so friendly I felt like I had known them all my life. Madge and I really hit it off. We must have stayed with them two or three nights. We were having such a good time we couldn't keep up with the time. They took us to festivals and introduced us to their friends in Louisiana. We also went to New Orleans with them. J took a picture of me peeping around the Bourbon Street sign on Bourbon Street. We were having so much fun they didn't want us to leave, and we really didn't want to go, but we had to move on to visit Dot and Dwayne. They were glad to see us. Dot and I had a lot in common and many things to talk about while J visited with Dwayne. We visited with them for a while, but we didn't spend the night. Our vacation time was moving on in a hurry. We went through some old antebellum houses and went to a plant where they made Tabasco sauce. J picked up a souvenir for me from each place we stopped. We did a lot of sightseeing. I sent postcards to both our moms and one to Buddy's mom and Gary. Our two-week vacation was coming to an end, but there would be many more. I enjoyed those trips so much since I always wanted to travel after being stuck in the same place for thirty-two years. We went home to the double-wide, and J went back to work at Shickel's. He is a machinist and a very good one. He has worked for them for forty-one years. He likes his job, and they like him.

CHAPTER FIFTY-NINE

After J and I got home from our vacation, I went to check on Mom. She was now eighty-nine years old and starting to have little accidents. Sometimes, I had to take her to the hospital. Fortunately, she didn't break any bones. I was worried about her all the time, and if she didn't answer her phone, I always thought that maybe she had fallen again. I asked her to move down with me and J, but she wasn't ready for that; she still wanted her independence. She visited us often, and she had a room of her own when she came, but she still wasn't ready to move in with us. I said, "What if we get you a mobile home and put it on our property?" I told her she wouldn't have to pay rent anymore, and she would still have her independence. Her rent in Harrisonburg went up about every year, and that didn't leave her much for food and medicine. She thought about that and agreed to do that. We went to many different places, looking for a mobile home for her. She just wanted us to get her a used one, but I told her that by the time we made all the repairs, we might as well get a new one. I had the search narrowed down to two places, and I finagled with them back and forth until Mom told me I was embarrassing her. Each one of the dealers wanted to make the sale, and I knew it, so I kept holding out. I finally settled on one costing $4,000 less than they were asking for it. After the deal was made, the owner told me that I had played that salesman like a fine-tuned guitar. Mom wanted a medicine cabinet, which wasn't in the mobile home, so I got them to throw that in too. The rest of it was beautifully furnished. The owner told me I had stolen that mobile home. It reminded me of my half brother telling me, "You stole those fish." The difference was that this time I knew what I was doing and so did the salesman, so it wasn't the same as stealing fish.

CHAPTER SIXTY

$\mathcal{M}$om lived in the mobile home for three years, at which time Sabrina came down and wanted her to move to Harrisonburg with her. Mom always loved Harrisonburg. Another factor was that Sabrina had three boys who kept Mom entertained. She dearly loved those boys, and Sabrina needed somebody to look after them while she was working. I told Mom I would keep the mobile home for a year in case she changed her mind and wanted to come back. I knew how she was, and she could never be happy in one place for long. If I had to sell the mobile home, I didn't want it to depreciate. We put her mobile home next to J's grandma's old house that we were planning to renovate. Our double-wide was just up the road so I could keep tabs on Mom while she lived there. After she went to live with Sabrina, I still picked her up once each week for her day out. If she was watching the boys, we took them with us. Mom had been with Sabrina maybe six months when she called and told me she was happy staying with Sabrina and I could go ahead and sell the mobile home. We put the mobile home on the market, and it sold right away. I made $1,000 more than I had paid for it after Mom lived in it for three years. The Lord was blessing us real good!

CHAPTER SIXTY-ONE

$\mathcal{M}$om stayed in Harrisonburg with Sabrina about two years and was very happy, but Sabrina and her husband wanted to buy a house. They were tired of renting. The only problem was, the house they were buying was in Stuarts Draft. Mom didn't like it there, so she went to live with my brother, Donnie, who lived in Waynesboro. She lived with him for a short period of time, but she didn't like Waynesboro either. One day, out of the blue, she called and wanted to come back with me. I had already sold the mobile home and didn't want to go down that road again. We were already in the process of restoring the old house. The old house was built in the 1800s. It was built of log, which had been hand hewn. It had beautiful wood upstairs in three of the rooms. J washed the wood with Clorox, and I sealed it with polyurethane. I also thought that since Mom was coming back, we would need another bathroom for her. She needed one all to herself because she could spend hours in the bathroom. Her bathroom was located right off the parlor. The parlor would become her living room and would be handy for her when she was downstairs. She was still getting around good at that time, so her bedroom was upstairs across the hall from us. There was also another bathroom in the middle of our bedroom and her bedroom if she needed to get up at night. That bathroom was mainly my bathroom. We all three had our separate bathrooms except at night when I shared mine. J had his bathroom downstairs.

CHAPTER SIXTY-TWO

We didn't have the house quite finished when Mom moved back. We had everything for her finished. We just didn't have the kitchen finished yet. We had picnics in the house before we finished the kitchen. She seemed to settle back in fine. I just had to wonder for how long. She surprised me because she was still here after about five years. She was beginning to get unsteady, so I got her a walker to try to help keep her steady, but she didn't like the walker and hardly ever used it. She had a real stubborn streak in her. If she didn't want to do something, she just didn't do it. I told her she needed to use it, especially when she got up from her nap. She was really unsteady then. This particular day, she was on our couch in our living room. As usual, she didn't take her walker with her. I took the walker in and told her when she got up from her nap to be sure to use it. After she went to sleep, I went upstairs to clean and make the bed. I was almost finished when I heard a big thud. I ran downstairs to find Mom on the floor. I called the rescue squad because I was afraid to move her. I didn't know how bad she was hurt. They took her to the hospital, and we got her checked out. She didn't have any broken bones, but the doctor wanted her to go to Life Care for a while for therapy. I went down every day to take her for rides in her wheelchair, and with the nurses' help, I brought her home for a little while. She was getting more dissatisfied at the nursing home all the time. Every day she was asking me to take her home. She was supposed to have therapy for six weeks, but she was getting so restless that she was trying to get out of bed and fell a couple of times. This bothered me because I thought she would undo all the progress she had made. The nursing home was a beautiful facility, and you would have thought she would do fine for six weeks. Most people would do fine for that period of time, but not Mom. She had to make waves. I talked to the nursing home staff, and they said she wasn't ready to go home yet. I knew it was no use to try to tell Mom that, so I asked them if I could give her therapy at home. I knew what they did, and I could do it at home and keep her happy. They reluctantly agreed to that, providing I had a trained therapist to come in to help out. I said that would be fine, so I took her home in four weeks instead of six. I would take her for a walk around the porch several times each day. She always had her walker, and I had a belt I put around her so I could catch her if she started to fall. At this time, I spent most of my time just caring for Mom. I quit my craftwork altogether. I picked up everything from the shops that they hadn't sold and just took care of Mom. By this time, it had become a full-time job. I had to get her a hospital bed and move her bedroom downstairs. She was also on oxygen. She didn't have to be on oxygen all the time, only when she got short of breath and during the night. Mom never walked again although she had the therapy. She had simply gotten too weak. She was now ninety-nine years old, and I had to take her in the wheelchair all the time. I also had to lift her from one place to the other all the time. She had gotten so restless she wanted to be moving all the time. I would no more than get her moved to one place when she would want to move again. Then I got her a motorized wheelchair so she could move whenever she wanted to, and I wouldn't have to lift her all the time. Gary and J wanted me to put her in a nursing home full-time because they could see what this was doing to me; however, I couldn't see it. The motorized chair didn't work out either because Mom never learned how to drive it, and she nearly wrecked our house in trying. If anything got in her way, she just ran over it if she could. She got the chair wedged in the doorway, and I had a terrible time getting her out of that fix. I just gave up on her driving, and when I wanted to take her outside, it was easier to use the motorized wheelchair instead of the regular chair I had to push. I would just walk beside her and drive her chair for her. As long as she had me with her all the time, she was happy.

CHAPTER SIXTY-THREE

I heard about a new facility called Generations Crossing. I thought if I could get Mom in there, it would give her something to do, and she would be with people going through the same thing that she was. If she could just get something to interest her, maybe she wouldn't be so restless all the time. She was accepted at Generations Crossing, which turned out to be one of the best moves I ever made. She fit right in. She learned to play dominos there, which turned out to be her favorite game. I never would have thought she would like dominos. It was her favorite game maybe because she won most of the time. They called her the domino queen since she was so good at it. They played a lot of games, but she wouldn't participate in anything else. We got G&W Ambulance service to pick her up in the morning and take her to school, as she called it. She celebrated her one hundredth birthday there. We had a party for her, and they had *The Daily News* write a story about her. They had a big story about her and pictures I didn't know they had taken until they came out in the paper. Going to Generations Crossing was about like a regular school, only it was for old people. She was very happy there and seemed very content, which was good to see. She looked forward to going every weekday of the week and stayed home on the weekend. This gave me time to run errands and get groceries and her medicine. Generations Crossing was the very best thing that could have happened for me or Mom. They had registered nurses there plus a lot of helpers. The nurses always took care of all their physical needs and also knew how to handle people with mental problems. They brought children in to visit the old people, which gave Mom a real lift. She missed Sabrina's boys so much and loved to see those kids. They loved her as well.

CHAPTER SIXTY-FOUR

All good things must come to an end, and so it was at Generations Crossing. Mom was getting so bad I was unable to send her anymore, but I was so glad she had this interest in playing dominos. She couldn't do much of anything for herself anymore, but she could still play dominos. I became her full-time partner, and she wanted to play all the time until she got so tired she was ready for a nap. She beat me at dominos most of the time, and I didn't just let her win. She actually beat me. She had calmed down from wanting to move all the time. We played dominos instead, which was much easier on me because I didn't have to lift her as much as I did before. When I put her in bed at night, I always put her oxygen on her. She used it at night but very seldom in the day. I got a baby monitor to take up to my bedroom so I could hear her if she got restless during the night and tried to get out of bed. I always put the rails up on the bed, but she would try to crawl out over them. Sometimes, she would wake up during the night and yell, "Let me out of here." I would go down and try to get her settled back in to sleep, but sometimes I would just have to get her out of bed and stay up with her. I put a fish aquarium in her room, which entertained her some of the time when she couldn't sleep. It had different kinds and colors, and it also served as a night-light. She would tell me if she thought one of the fish was missing. They were usually just hiding, and when I pointed that out to her, she was satisfied.

CHAPTER SIXTY-FIVE

Sabrina came to see Mom. She was living in Georgia at that time. She didn't get to see Mom very often. Mom also got to see her grandsons. She was so happy to have them around her. She missed Sabrina and the boys. I don't know just how it came about, but Mom wanted to go to Georgia with Sabrina. I'm sure she didn't realize what a long trip it would be, but she was determined she was going. I was afraid the trip would be too much for her in the condition she was in, and I tried to talk her out of the whole thing. She was getting very hard to reason with, and when she wanted to do something, she wouldn't listen to reason. All she could think about was being with Sabrina and the boys. She insisted on going no matter what else a trip like that would require. Sabrina said she would take good care of her, but I was still reluctant about her going. I knew how much Sabrina and the boys loved her, and I knew they would take good care of her, but a lot of things had changed since she stayed with Sabrina before. I knew she would be a handful for Sabrina since she hadn't seen how much attention Mom needed. She hadn't been around here for a while, and as far as she could see, Mom hadn't changed that much. She looked great, but she was far from being as good as she looked. I also had Mom in diapers, which needed to be changed. I had to brush her teeth, comb her hair, bathe her, and take care of open wounds from the least little bump. It was really a full-time job. I didn't know Sabrina was still working and wouldn't be with her full-time just like I was. Mom loved Sabrina so very much, and Sabrina felt the same way about her. As it turned out, instead of Mom taking care of the boys, they were taking care of her to the best of their ability. Sabrina had worked when Mom was with her before, but this time was a much different story. One of the boys was always there, but they couldn't meet Mom's needs. Sabrina cared for her in the evening. She bathed her and did everything that was required in the evening, but during the day, she was somewhat on her own. It was only a matter of days when I called to see how Mom was doing. I was still thinking that Sabrina was with her all the time. Sabrina put Mom on the phone, and she started crying and told me the situation there, and she wanted me to go get her. I knew that wouldn't be easy. I thought about renting a van to take her home, but then I remembered my brother, Donnie, had a motor home with a bed that we could use to take Mom home. I was sure it would be too hard on her in a car since she had just made that long trip to get there. I called Donnie and told him what was going on and asked him if he would take me to get Mom if I paid all the expenses. He said he needed a little vacation and readily agreed to help me. J drove me to Waynesboro to Donnie's house to meet him, and Donnie and I were on our way to Georgia. We drove all the way to Sabrina's, only stopping long enough to get gas. We had packed snacks, so we were fine. When we walked into Sabrina's, Mom's face lit up like a Christmas tree. She knew she was going home. Donnie said we would go ahead and start for home and stop for the night at a camping area. I got us some substantial food. I knew Mom needed more than snacks. I slept in the bed with Mom, and Donnie was in the other room. None of us got any sleep because Mom wouldn't settle down and kept yelling "Help me." I was doing all I possibly could to make her comfortable, but it was dark, and she didn't know where she was and she was afraid. I knew this would be hard on Donnie since he had to drive home with no sleep, but he said that was the only thing to do because he couldn't sleep anyhow with Mom constantly yelling. Mom seemed to relax some and stopped yelling after we were moving again. When daylight came, Mom was doing better, and we were able to make it back to Donnie's house. I had already called J to pick us up, and he was at Donnie's by the time we got there. I kept Mom for about two more years after that. She was doing pretty good in those two years, but then she took a turn for the worst, and we had to put her in the hospital. She was so sick we didn't think she was going to make it, but she was a tough cookie and she started getting better. Gary and J still wanted me to put her in a nursing home. I thought this was possibly the best thing to do at this time since I was so worn out and I was worried that if something happened to me first, I didn't know how J would be able to cope with things.

CHAPTER SIXTY-SIX

$\mathcal{I}$ called Sabrina, and she came home to help me with everything. We visited all the nursing homes around Harrisonburg, but none of them were suitable as far as Sabrina and I were concerned. I really wanted her to go to VMRC. I had tried to get her in respite care one time when J and I wanted to go on vacation for a while, but they had no room for her. At that time, I put her name on the list for respite care. Sabrina and I went to VMRC and talked to the people there about getting Mom in, but they were full. It was very hard to get into VMRC. I just started praying that the Lord would make a way for us. The doctor knew we had to do something about getting her in a home, so he set up a place for her to go to one of the other nursing homes. The evening before she was to go to the nursing home the doctor had set up, I got a call from VMRC when I got home from the hospital. They told me they had a place for Mom at VMRC. I said, "Thank you, Lord!" He is so faithful to make a way where there seems to be no way. The next morning, I went to the hospital to find the doctor and the people from the other nursing home there. I told the doctor that Mom wasn't going to that nursing home. He had an uneasy look on his face as though he couldn't believe what I had just told him. He said, "What? Where is she going?" I told him VMRC. He said, "How did you get her in there?" I pointed up and said, "I didn't. He did." He fully understood what I was saying, and he sent the people back to their nursing home. This is what I had been praying for and trusting God to bring it about. I was just thanking and praising God for the answer to my prayer. I got G&W to take Mom to the nursing home, and I met them there. After Sabrina saw that Mom was going to make it, she went back home, but she sure helped me while she was here. Mom didn't want me to leave, but I assured her I would be there early in the morning. I went in the next morning to find that her roommate kept the curtains pulled all the time, and Mom thought she was alone in the room. Mom needed to see somebody so she wouldn't feel alone. Again, the Lord worked it all out for us. There was a lady who lived about two doors up from Mom's room. She asked if Mom wanted to be her roommate. Her name was Mary. She had been a schoolteacher and was a very pleasant person. I accepted right away, and Mom and Mary never closed the curtains between them. Mom and Mary got along real well. I would go in each day and take them to all the different things they had going on at the home. They were both in wheelchairs. I would push one and pull the other. They were both enjoying all the things they had going on at the home. One thing Mom liked to do was go to the spa on spa day. She just loved to be pampered. She had her fingernails done and picked out her own color. There were also college students who went to the home to do things for the residents. They did whatever the residents wanted them to do.

Mom always got her fingernails done. There was a beauty shop on Main Street in the home where I would take Mom once each week to get her hair done. During this time, J and I were looking for a church to go to. We weren't able to go when we had Mom all the time. We settled on Mount Olive where Sonny Henkel was the pastor. You could tell Sonny was a man of God. Sonny's wife, Myrna, played the piano, and I must say she played it very well. We immediately fell in love with the people there. They were all so friendly, and we seemed to fit right in. Sonny and Myrna went to the nursing home to see Mom, and Sonny played dominos with her. He even got her a stand to hold her dominos. Every time Sonny went to see her, she would tell the nurses, "That was Maxine's preacher." She really enjoyed seeing Sonny go to see her. He was extra special to her. He also sang to her. Sonny has a wonderful voice, and he just made her day. He is blessed with so many talents. He went to see her often.

CHAPTER SIXTY-SEVEN

$\mathcal{M}$om celebrated her 102nd birthday at the home. She was still doing pretty well mentally. She could still play dominos with anybody who would play with her. I had a 102nd birthday party for her at the home. The nurses, Donnie, and two of my first cousins were there. She had a ball with all the attention she was getting. She just loved that attention! I also had her 103rd birthday there, but by this time, she was getting weaker and slept most of the time. She always knew who Mary was and she knew me and J, but she was beginning to get a little confused now. One Saturday, J and I went to see her, and she told me she had gone to Penny's and charged some books on my account, so we would have to go pay them. I used to charge things for her all the time when I took her shopping on her day out. I realized that she was going back in time and confusing the past with the present. I just went along with whatever she said. She told me to get her pocketbook for her. She didn't have any at the home, so I gave her mine. She said, "That's not my pocketbook." She kept insisting that we go pay for those books she had charged, so J and I took her up to Main Street at the home where they had some little shops and pretended to pay for her books. She was satisfied with that. I knew she wouldn't be with us much longer. I told Mary I hope she made it to her 103rd birthday. She made that, and then I told Mary I hope she can live just three more months, at which time she would be 103 and three months to the day. Mom passed away on the twenty-fifth of April 2006. When J and I went to the home to pick up her things, Mary said, "You got your wish. She lived the next three months." Mary was a good Christian lady, and she knew God had granted me that request. Sonny preached at her funeral. I continued to go see Mary. She didn't have a family close by, and I knew she would be very lonely without Mom. Most of her family lived in West Virginia. I didn't go every day to see Mary, but I went two or three times each week. I called before I went to see if she felt like taking a ride in her wheelchair to the bargain center, or just stay in the room and talk. Mary had bone cancer, and she had already lived seventeen years beyond the time the doctors had given her. She was such a blessing to everyone. She would read to the residents who were blind and do anything she could do to help them. Mary loved to go to the bargain center. I used to take both her and Mom there. If she wanted to do other things and felt up to it, she would tell the nurses in advance to have her ready to go because I would be going and would be taking her places. They had her ready by the time I got there. The nurses told me Mary always looked forward to my visits. Mary always looked after Mom at night if she got restless and rang for the nurses because Mom couldn't do that for herself. I really appreciated all Mary did for her, and I told her so. Mary was very mentally sound. Mary lived to the following January after Mom died. I think she was praying she could live longer than Mom did so she could help her. Mary was a wonderful lady! Mary was sent to the hospital because she was going downhill fast. The last time J and I went to see her, she told me she didn't think she was going to make it this time. She didn't make it on earth, but I am assured that Mom and Mary are both with Jesus. We went to Mary's funeral. She was loved by everybody who had ever known her. One thing we all know for sure is that this life is not final. We haven't even begun to live here on earth; our real life will be our eternal life. We will be free from all pain and sorrow. Praise the Lord!

END

J. and cars 156

J. and cars 157

J. and cars 160

SNAPSHOTS

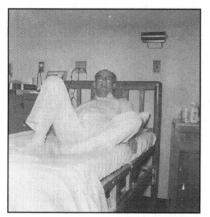
Daddy in hospital

Maxine 2 years old

Mom and Dad on car

Maxine 10 and
Donnie 12

Maxine 3 years old

Maxine 5 and
Donnie 7

I have had the pleasure of knowing Maxine because we attend church together. I admire her Christian Faith and see how it has helped her to cope with her on-going fight against cancer. Maxine has a bright and positive out look on life and is prepared for its trials and tribulations through her faith in our Lord.

Her thoughtfulness towards others impresses me as well. As an example, when I was visiting her in the hospital, she looked at her watch and said she needed to call Jay to bring some things from home when he came to visit that evening. I said can't you call him on his cell phone? Her reply was that she worried about him driving and answering his phone, as she did not feel this was a safe thing to do. (I wish more people felt that way!). She was waiting for the exact moment that she knew he would be home and walking into their kitchen.

I feel blessed to call Maxine my friend.

Pearl Castle

Pearl

Maxine 8 and
Donnie 10

Maynard and Jean

Maxine and Buddy

Grandma Snow and Gary

Donnie and Walter

Maxine Connie and Jim

Issac & Margaret Vanpelt
Roadcap

Grandma & Uncle Minor

Maxine 4 years old

Earman Roadcap

Mother Dorcas Roadcap Father Link Roadcap... Link had a brother named Zebedee and
Zebedee had a daughter named Ponnie. Ponnie was very mentally challenged... Daddy
had a brother named Minor. He was mentally challenged too, but not as bad as Ponnie.
They tried to send Uncle Minor to school, but that didn't work out very well .Uncle Minor
stuttered very bad and his teacher was trying to get him to read the word glass. She asked
him what he had in his windows at home. She was hoping that would give him a clue. He
said "PA pa papa's old pants. Daddy told me this story. Then the teacher thought she would
try spelling. She asked him to spell milk. He said milkg. If only he had left off the G.   They
were having a Christmas program at church and they gave Uncle Minor the shortest verse
in the Bible. Jesus wept. When it was Uncle Minor's turn, He said "God cried" He had a pet
pigeon, I saw this myself. Uncle Minor played the French harp and he played it very well.
The pigeon would get up and strut around to the sound of the music. Daddy had another
brother named Guy. Guy married Nellie. And that union produced a daughter named Rita
Lee, and a daughter named Lavonne. They also had a son named Udell. Daddy had a sister
named Dilly she married Charlie Lam. From this union came James Lam, Sidney, Leonard,
Charlotte, Helen, Mildred, Wilda, Ava, Frankie, Kirby John, Delmar and Cora.   Daddy
also had a brother named John. Uncle john Married Aunt Daisy. We were closer to them
than the rest of our uncles and Aunts From this union came Ruth, Doris, Gloria, Jean, John
Jr., Joe, and Bobby.

Ancestry

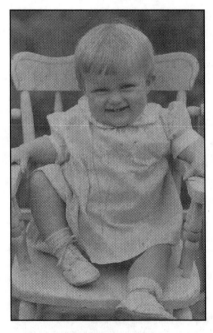

Scanmaxine 15   roadcap grandparents

Mom 100 years old

Mom 101 years old

Mom 102 years old

Mom 103 years old

older than dirt

Santa Claus and Cutie Bear

Mom and Dad

J. and Maxine Wedding

J. and Maxine Wedding 2

J. and Maxine Wedding 3

J. and Maxine Wedding 4

J. and Maxine Wedding 5

Mom and Maxine

Boy at the pond

Midnight at pond

Big Pond

Cokie and Misty

Cokie

Panda cake

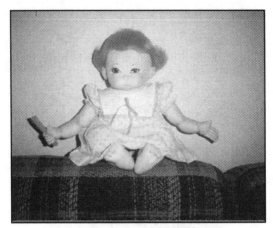

Doll crafted by Maxine

Deer crafted by Maxine

Our House at Christmas

Maxine at Word Ministries

Maxine and Misty

Maxine at Lake Charles Lousiana

Maxine and Buddy after he got sick

Maxine and Gary in Ridge

Fort Hood Texas

Gary, Misty & pigs

Misty

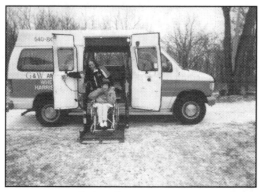

Mama coming home from Generations Crossing

Three pictures of J.